EXODUS

a roadmap for the centre-left

© 2018 Henrik Sass Larsen

Publish: BoD – Books on Demand, Copenhagen, Denmark

Print: BoD – Books on Demand, Norderstedt, Germany

ISBN: 9788743002192

CONTENTS

A common refrain met me at every turn when I told the people in my life that I was writing a book: "Don't do it!"

How in the world could an MP and member of the party's top brass write a book to spark political debate amongst a public constantly on the lookout for the seeds of tomorrow's furore – without damaging his party or his own standing? Call it imprudent if you will, but here it is.

In the process of writing this book, I have had frequent conversations with those around me about staying in tune with the party's core political positions, while securing their blessings when charting a maverick course on other, less integral fronts.

Such is life as a member of a political party and an individual. You can't agree on everything, but it's also unfeasible if you disagree on matters at the heart of the party. Thank you to my fellow party leaders for accompanying me in this journey. I have drawn heavily on your input, learned much, and embraced your excellent advice.

And thank you to all those who warned me that most of the content in this book can be misused by the press, who may present isolated passages to fellow MPs and other party members as fodder for reports of internal discord on policy. The majority of you also thought that publishing this book was worth the effort nonetheless – opting not to do so would be acquiescing to journalistic tyranny.

Thanks to Mette Frederiksen for good advice and feedback. Thanks to Martin Rossen for many long talks on subjects far and wide. Thanks to Martin Justesen for support of all kinds. Thanks to Peter Strauss Jørgensen, Morten Høyer, Andreas Gylling Æbelø, Sten Kristensen, Thor Möger Pedersen, Sara Vad Sørensen, Dan Jørgensen, Nicolai Wammen and Peter Hummelgaard Thomsen for your contributions and critical acumen.

And special thanks to David Erritzøe, who sought to teach me about the world of drugs – I strongly emphasise that he can in no way be held accountable for the contents of this book. And thanks to all of you who risked the obliteration of your good reputations if it ever emerged that you had advised in connection with this book.

Thanks to Ørselv Kloster for ideal writing conditions.

Thanks to Hanne Malmborg for commas and comments. Thanks to Morgan Krüger for research. Thanks to AIA for many good contributions.

Thanks to my little family, Susanne and Nynne, who

so often must bear the burden of seeing me discussed in the media and defending me.

And thanks to the Social Democratic Party for a life-long and loving stay.

NEW CENTRE-LEFT

INTRODUCTION

This is a debate piece on the centre-left. In the following, centre-left refers to all of the social democratically-minded parties near the centre and common sense, and at a good distance from the extreme socialist fringes. It is through the strength and positions of these parties that an alternative to populism, conservatism and liberalism must be forged and honed. Those currently revelling in the drastic left turns such as those in Britain's Labour Party are doing so in vain. The Marxist ghosts of the past are not worth revisiting.

For the centre-left to once more become a societal pillar of cohesion and development, we must build on the best of what we have achieved thus far. Given their success in building welfare and securing broad political solutions, Europe's post-WWII social democratic parties offer a useful blueprint, as do reform governments such as New Labour.

But to continue in these footsteps, the centre-left must formulate a relevant political platform for today's issues and challenges. The absence of a relevant policy on immigration and globalisation has been a glaring failure of the centre-left throughout most of the Western world, leading to the utter decimation of time-honoured parties. This book examines and proposes policies on immigration, globalisation, the public sector, the public discussion, business, drugs, and Israel, and lays out why centre-left ideology is the best political idea of all time. It is not perfect and it is not complete, but rather a mission to be carried on to fruition by those who pick up the torch. And, of course, countless intriguing topics remain untouched by this book – topics which others would be far more suited to discuss. This is a proposal on how the centre-left can return to relevance.

Some of us have been given the honour of leading a magnificent and longstanding party for a time. It is our undeniable duty to care for the party to the best of our abilities, while guiding its evolution and adaptation to the world of today. The best advice of many would be to play it defensively and hope that wear and tear on the other side will eventually open the door for the centre-left once more. They may be correct. On the other hand, leading a government without a carefully planned platform and purely due to the incompetence of others is a tepid political ambition. The goal must be a centre-left that uplifts, shapes and defines society. This is the ambition of the New Centre-Left.

OUR IDEOLOGICAL FOUNDATION

Freedom, equality and solidarity

What makes a person happy? The answers are many, but rarely is "politics" amongst the unsolicited answers. The notion that politics and political choices could make people happy would hardly garner much applause in any forum, while the opposite view – that poor political choices, poor political administration and poor politicians make people unhappy – would likely earn a much higher approval rating.

The answer is that politics – exercising power – can create the framework for people to be happy, and for them to be unhappy.

Around the world, people offer their lives in the fight for the right to vote – and thus for a share of power. And around the world, a host of maniacs fight to impose their interpretation of a happy life on others – or rather, they usually fight to put their own well-being first, at the expense of most.

Politics is a battle about means, prosperity, distribution, morality and souls – about hopes, tragedies, abuses, crimes, generosity and our limited collective resources. All these ingredients play a part in determining whether we achieve a decent and happy life. Thus politics is important and ever-relevant. As long as people walk the Earth, we will have to relate to life from a political perspective. There is no correct design, nor a key at the end of a book with all the answers. Our surroundings are constantly changing, thereby changing the basis and conditions for political choices. Politics is – and will remain – an integral condition of human existence, thereby rendering the decision-making parties and politicians all the more interesting. A party hoping to survive in the long term must base its politics on an ideology. A timeless and all-encompassing idea. An idea which can provide a direction and meaning in any age, and in the light of any technological, cultural or social developments. The centre-left builds on such an ideology: democratic socialism.

Democratic socialism rests on three pillars: freedom, equality and solidarity.

Freedom is the presence of dignified options for the individual.

Equality is equal rights and obligations.

Solidarity is unpersonified compassion for others.

FREEDOM

Freedom is the presence of dignified options for the individual.

Human history is a story largely devoid of freedom. From archaeological studies of prehistoric times, we know that a scarcity of food combined with disease made life difficult and inhibited freedom. Throughout the history of civilisation, the scarcity of food alone has made life difficult for most people. Even today, despite the overwhelming biological success of humanity, millions still live on the brink of starvation.

When you're hungry and don't have the money or the means to fill your stomach, you are not free. Scavenging for roots in the earth or, for that matter, scouring through mountains of waste to find food has nothing to do with freedom – despite the fact that libertarians would likely define these people as free because their tax burden is next to nothing.

Unfortunately, political structures throughout the history of civilisation have largely entailed a dearth of freedom. Charming examples of tribal societies and small civilisations with a minimum of political oppression certainly exist, but societies have predominantly rested on the principle of all power and privilege to the strongest. Military victors became political leaders, calling themselves kings, emperors, etc – and usually imposing widespread oppression and exploitation of the populace for their own benefit.

These societies also lacked freedom, despite the edict of various conservative parties through the ages that royalty and nobility are god-given.

And speaking of God: for some reason, people throughout history have sought to make sense of existence through a religion typically affiliated with the local rulers and at times rivalling military dictators in their oppressive fervour. A god-given and thus predestined religion sets no person free – quite the contrary. This is what makes an interpretation of Islam as religious law so incompatible with a society where religion has been secularised for hundreds of years.

The prerequisites for freedom are access to sufficient resources, the freedom to choose the powers that be, and freedom from the religious doctrine of predestination.

The industrial revolution and the technologies ensuing in its wake have enabled the production of sufficient resources. We can now produce so much food that no one should starve. But distribution is another matter altogether.

Through assorted democratic reforms over the past 150 years, most European nations have successfully established true democracy, with populations able to elect and depose political leaders.

In a slow process beginning with the Renaissance, science and private life have managed to escape the suffocating grasp of religious morality.

The basic prerequisites for freedom are in place.

But, of course, this is a very superficial perspective. Rather than a homage to the progress of freedom, European history of the past 100 years is a long and tragic parade of setbacks, war, violence and persecution. The cornerstones of today's freedoms are awash in bloodshed at the hands of Nazis, fascists and communists – atrocities driven by the worst of humanity, exacting a price paid primarily by Jews and young Americans and Brits who died for this cause. In an odd twist of fate, many of the angry young people who sometimes demonstrate against the United States have almost only the United States to thank for the freedom to do so.

But freedom is more than basic prerequisites.

TRUE FREEDOM

Do a full stomach, the right to vote and freedom from religious intervention constitute a sufficient formula for freedom? For much of the right wing, the answer to this question is yes.

For the centre-left, the answer is no.

Historically, the centre-left has been responsible for expanding true freedom to include three major freedom projects: work, education and health.

No person is free without access to a job.

Photographs from the 1930s depict unemployed men standing in long lines, hoping to get work for just one day. There is very little or no aid available to them. Unemployment has skyrocketed as a result of the Great Depression. And waiting back home are families suffering from the lack of income. Doing something about this situation became the number one freedom project of the labour movement.

Working – and thereby generating an income for oneself and one's family – is a fundamental right. Dignity is the product of a job that is tolerable and even desirable, with a yield that is sufficient for a decent existence for oneself and one's family. Thus the rise of labour unions that ensure decent pay and working

16

conditions. Thus the freedom to obtain an education and the freedom to apply for a wide range of jobs. Freedom is access to income compensation in the event of unemployment.

Freedom is having the opportunity to study, regardless of social and economic background.

In the past, the story was that if you were born in the working class, then you remained part of the working class. The opportunity and prospect of obtaining a higher education was largely non-existent prior to the welfare society of the 1960s. Regardless of how talented and industrious you were, your social background determined your future.

Breaking these chains became the second major freedom project of the centre-left.

If there are insurmountable economic barriers to getting an upper secondary, vocational or university education, then you do not have freedom. Thus the reason for educational grants, equal and free university access for all students, and the education guarantee for vocational students.

Freedom is also having the best available health care, regardless of social and economic background. If you have to haggle with an insurance company about your right to decent and full treatment for your illness, then you are not free, and if you are denied such treatment, you are ill off. When somebody is turned away at the door to a private hospital because of an inability to pay, the lack of freedom and justice is clear – at least, that is, to the centre-left.

Freedom is the presence of dignified options for the individual – in every significant aspect of life. Without access to work, education and health, there is no true freedom.

EQUALITY

Equality is equal opportunities and obligations

The political history of humankind is one long struggle for freedom. A struggle to achieve freedom through equal rights. It is a struggle bathed in blood, be it that of the poorest serf or the modern-day soldier. Equal rights are so important that they are worth dying for.

Equal political rights have been at the forefront of this struggle. Equal and free choice for all adult citizens is a simple and – one would think – reasonable demand. Yet in 2018, this is still not customary around the world. Democracy is found in many incomplete versions; meanwhile, the most populated nations are governed by authoritarian means, and the right to vote is not a matter of course. Young people who have grown up in a secure and free material western life must sometimes be forced to look up from the entertainment of iPads and witness the international news, so as to realise that their world could be much different – and, hopefully, to be shocked by what they see.

The centre-left in European countries has led the charge for equal political rights. This includes voting rights for workers, servants and the poor – a right they had been denied by conservative forces. Women's suffrage was also a key cause of the centre-left, as was the right of young adults to vote. Through more than 100 years of struggle, these battles have been won in spite of the right wing, which in most cases is left with nothing but the shame of being on the wrong side of history.

There have been plenty of frontal attacks on political rights hard earned through struggle – from Franco's fascists, to Hitler's Nazis and the long, oppressive reign of the communists in Eastern Europe. Driven by a hunger for power, Russia began spreading the plague of nationalism to easternmost Europe in 2015, undermining political civil rights; meanwhile, an ever-more radicalised version of Islam is being practised in the Middle East, whose population is oppressed in the name of religion. It is this version of Islam that many immigrants from the Middle East have brought with them to Europe. Democracy is by no means a given – it must be protected and fought for.

Political equality is a necessary component of true freedom, but it is not sufficient in and of itself. You can have the right to vote but live in such absurd poverty or misery that this right is largely meaningless.

And so it follows that economic equality is a prerequisite for a sustainability equality and freedom.

If a very small number of people, a royal family or an exotic gangster have stockpiled the majority of a nation's wealth, the resulting inequality constitutes a massive and grotesque divide between rich and poor. This is because wealthy people rarely have a stop button. They incessantly seek the accumulation of more and more resources for themselves, and they typically have no social qualms in this pursuit. History is ripe with examples of the vulgar splendour and exhibitionist lifestyle of kings, while their subjects are literally starving at the castle gates.

Local dictators around the world continue to take this shameless approach – take Africa for example, which offers many examples of such disheartening behaviour over the past 50 years. However, similar stories are to be found on every continent. And the most depressing thing of all is that the progress of yesteryear is being dismantled in the English-speaking part of the world, where inequality is accelerating at breakneck speed.

The instrument for fighting economic inequality – while financing collective welfare in the process – is a just tax system.

The state and a progressive income tax system have been used to achieve greater economic equality and justice. Nearly all industrialised Western countries have gone from barbaric social and economic conditions to welfare states with greater income distribution. In this process, the wealth and influence of the pre-industrial giants and entrenched ruling class was decimated, and the working class became the middle class. A unique centre-left vision was realised through the creation of the welfare society, with one of the key methods being progressive taxation and extensive income distribution.

An effective and equalising taxation of incomes and wealth is a prerequisite for ensuring that the few do not hoard all the wealth. Just taxation is the number one enemy of the right wing (when they're not busy meddling in what goes on in people's bedrooms). For them, the income or wealth that you accumulate or inherit is a private matter into which society should intervene as little as possible. The centre-left has a multifaceted response to such a view: To begin with, people can rarely accumulate such massive income without the contribution of others, by which reasoning something has gone intrinsically wrong in distributing the value of this work; or, if the income is solely achieved through speculation on capital, the underlying products or consumers are the actual payers; or, if one inherits significant resources, the lack of proper taxation is problematic.

Can you have a high income and great wealth in a social democratic vision of equality? Yes, you can. It could even be argued that the existence of the social democratic welfare society and its many consumers with significant income is absolutely essential to the growing cadre of billionaires.

Economic equality must be measured in terms of whether those at the bottom of the income distribution scale have a decent income that enables them to provide for themselves and their families, and whether those in the upper income class receive a proportional income corresponding to their efforts and pay a fair taxation on this income.

SOLIDARITY

Solidarity is unpersonified compassion for others

Giving a gift – be it to a young child or an elderly grandmother – fills the hearts of most people with joy. It feels good to give a gift, as the recipient usually expresses thankfulness ranging from the spontaneous glee of the child to the more restrained gratitude of the grandmother. And for the vast majority of people, it feels good and right to help a neighbour with shovelling snow from their pavement if needed, or to help a colleague at work by taking an extra shift because her child is ill with a throat infection.

When we have close personal contact, we are able to see and feel the results of our choosing to give something to somebody.

The equation is more nebulous when dealing with an entire society. Having compassion and giving something on that scale demands the organisational capacity of the public sector. And, inevitably, the element of personal contact is lost.

The project of the centre-left is to maintain these contributions and the willingness to give via the state and taxation.

Marianne – a 43-year-old woman who lives in the town of Horsens who you will never meet – has been diagnosed with breast cancer. Making it through the tribulations of cancer is difficult enough for her and her family. You and me and all the rest of us come into the picture by being thankful and proud that a publicly funded health care service provides Marianne with excellent treatment that will hopefully help her survive.

Face-to-face solidarity thus becomes the unpersonified compassion for others. In all respects, this is the purpose of the social democratic welfare state.

You could even claim that participation in this welfare state is profitable for each individual citizen. Even if you don't like to give, there are advantages to participating.

For those who can't stand the thought of sharing a hospital and a ward room with Marianne, the above scenario is obviously not to their liking; they would prefer private insurance and private hospitals where their needs – and their needs alone – are met. Under this model, Marianne and many like her are not guaranteed insurance, and therefore will not receive the necessary, high quality treatment that a collective insurance system can give her. Although one could claim that it is perfectly possible to have a collective health care service and give people the option of spending their own money on private solutions, the reality is that those who choose the private option will often demand exemption from helping to finance the collective system.

The unpersonified compassion for others applies to health care, and it applies to education and social conditions. Solidarity is also the joy of knowing that a young person has the freedom to get an education regardless of their personal savings or parents' income.

To mitigate the most extreme miseries, a society must not doom the individual to begging for alms, but instead uphold human dignity in the midst of a difficult social situation.

The lack of a job and the ability to provide for yourself and your family is tremendously humiliating for many people. Providing an economic safety net that enables the individual and the family to avoid financial ruin and get back on their feet is at the heart of a decent labour market policy.

Some people's lives are toppled by a physical handicap, and they need a hand from society to help them help themselves; others suffer mental illnesses, sometimes accompanied by various forms of substance abuse, which can render elementary daily tasks and routines unmanageable.

The common thread running through every case is that a decent society does not banish these people to the streets and leave them to their own devices, but instead helps those who unfortunately encounter such challenges in life. Our ability to give without forcing people to beg is our proud way of running a society founded on solidarity.

A balance must be struck between individuals providing for the needs of themselves and their families, while still having the ability to give to meet the collective needs of society. The formula was long ago described and defined through the realisation of the welfare state, although the specific details of its layout are constantly evolving.

"Forward" and "Continuing Forward" have been longstanding slogans of the social democratic movement. The creation of something new and better in society, and the goal that one's children should have a better life than one's own are inalienable objectives. The belief in progress – and the will to achieve it – fuel the political engine.

Collective societal projects are important, as are those of the individual. A central component of these projects is mutual respect between people. Some may shoot for the stars and become Hollywood celebrities, some may study theoretical physics and win the Nobel Prize, and some may earn a spot as a footballer in a Premier League squad. These are all outstanding accomplishments, and they are truly exceptional – because only very few will ever achieve them.

Yet people set goals in virtually every aspect of our society – goals of varying strength, scope and ambition. For some, this means getting an education; for others, it means saving up to buy a holiday home, or having a good family life. People appreciate and value things differently. The political task is to pave the way for people to achieve their realistic goals. In this way, each individual can strive to achieve what they view as a good and perhaps happy life.

If all these differences are to coalesce ideally in a society, it is essential that we respect the choices of others, while also ensuring that everyone contributes according to their abilities to the part of life that is collective.

What we do well today, we must do better tomorrow – be it at work, in the structuring of the public sector, or in our private spheres. We believe that the ambitious individual is the basis for an even better society, and that the optimum conditions for success are provided by a society that systematises freedom, equality and solidarity: the social democratic society.

LOVE IT OR ...

It's the number.

This is the one thing that all those who want to see the centre-left lead their country must learn to understand and accept as a fundamental premise. If you don't understand that the number of immigrants is the key to understanding why we have massive integration problems, then the chances that the population will bestow the centre-left with power anywhere are fortunately small.

Throughout the old Western world, massive immigration has led to extensive social, economic, political and cultural tensions. Whether it's in the Netherlands, France, the UK or Sweden, local and regional collapses of the welfare society are a reality in 2017. There are areas outside the rule of law, and there are areas where young new citizens grow up without being able to speak the language of their country, and whose physical and spiritual loyalty lies somewhere outside of Europe.

The number of immigrants in some parts of Europe is so high that the population development in certain regions will make the original citizens the minority. Europe has opened its doors to refugees and immigrants in the name of humanism. On the brink of collapse from this burden, Europe is now at risk of abandoning its values such as humanism in pure self-defence. These measures will ultimately diminish welfare societies due to the financial burden and limit freedoms because of the new security concerns caused by immigration from Muslim countries.

Immigration has been a disaster for Europe. All classical parties have a shared responsibility for this, especially the centre-left. The centre-left must accept this responsibility and then begin to correct its approach.

The principle must be as follows:

A country must only accept the number of refugees and immigrants that it can successfully integrate within a manageable period of time. The rest must be helped and supported elsewhere.

THERE IS A DIFFERENCE BETWEEN IMMIGRANTS

Many people once believed that time solves and resolves habits, customs and loyalty. They thought that, as the years passed, newcomers would adopt the fundamental values on which their new home country was built. Learn the language and its many nuances. Contribute new input and customs that the old tribe would embrace. Kiss, date and marry freely – and, after a couple of generations, be born and raised as equal citizens.

That conclusion was erroneous.

Or, rather, it is true enough for some groups of immigrants, but it was a huge miscalculation as regards the region producing the most immigrants.

Political etiquette has forbidden the division of immigrants according to their origin and religious affiliation.

Whether they hailed from the United States or Lebanon, an immigrant was an immigrant.

And that couldn't be further from the truth.

Immigrants with a western background have a relatively easy time with living and integrating in their new home. However, the opposite is true of immigrants and refugees with a Middle Eastern/Islamic background.

Be it Turks, Kurds, Somalis, Palestinians, or Iraqis, there are massive problems with integrating these people into society. Employment is low, especially for women. A disproportionate share are on public benefits. Low education levels – even for the third generation born and raised in the country. Significantly higher crime. Poorly functioning local communities in terms of day care institutions, schools, associations and the general sense of safety and security.

Throughout the Western world, you see one example after another showing that something is wrong with the integration of these groups of immigrants. And, unfortunately, there are very few positive examples.

Acknowledging that there is a difference between who you let into the country is a crucial premise and is closely linked with how many people can be successfully integrated. Refusing to acknowledge this now will mean opening our eyes at a later date and discovering an escalating integration disaster.

Why does it go wrong with Middle Eastern immigrants?

In the early 1970s, Denmark received a few thousand

Vietnamese boat refugees. At the same time, thousands of so-called "guest workers" arrived in the country, many of them from Turkey.

They took up residence in the same neighbourhoods. Attended the same schools and day care institutions and were offered the exact same opportunities for a free education.

Forty years later, we can see that their success has differed enormously. Practically all of the Vietnamese are employed, they have successfully established a life in the new country, they're virtually absent from crime statistics, and they have spread out and live in all parts of the country.

The Turks have a high unemployment rate. A lot of them are on social benefits. They're overrepresented in crime statistics and many of them still live in the same social housing where they were placed in the 1970s.

The difference in this development must be rooted in each group's approach to integration – the culture of each group.

Are you just visiting temporarily? If so, there's a certain type of behaviour and approach we expect of you. This includes observing the nation's laws and, for the sake of your family and general planning, knowing when you're returning home. In return, we will lessen our expectations in terms of language and integration.

Are you here to live permanently? That's another matter altogether. Then we actually demand that you integrate and become an active part of Danish society. That you do your duty before you demand your rights, and that you make sure to raise your family so that they can succeed in Danish society. That you observe the nation's laws, learn our language, embrace the values on which our democracy is built, and make your contribution to the society and the country to which you have moved. That you are loyal to your new home.

And this is where there are great doubts regarding the attitude and approach of many immigrant groups. To whom and what are they actually loyal?

The following example many seem one-sided, but since football is a very emotional matter for those involved, here it goes: During a friendly football match between the Danish and Turkish national sides in Copenhagen, there were more Turkish fans than Danish fans, but they were practically all Danish. The loyalty amongst these people, many of whom were born and raised in Denmark, is with a country they or their parents left long ago. For people who love football, such a manifestation arouses astonishment and great consternation. It begs at least two questions: Why did they leave the country that they support? Why in the world don't they root for the country of their birth, the country that gave them shelter?

In parts of Denmark you will find Turkish communities that speak with adoration of Erdogan's AKP party, and some are even members. Their view of Israel and the United States is typically very critical, if not hateful. In their living rooms, the satellite dish is tuned into Al Jazeera or other Middle Eastern media. In large parts of the Middle Eastern immigrant community, people focus their attention on the current agenda and news in the Middle East. Their loyalty is channelled more in that direction than towards the western democracy and welfare society in which they live.

Various Muslim circles and associations residing in western countries often use their time and energy to expound on how wonderful it would be to live according to Sharia law. Seen from the outside, this can be rather astounding, since the most common reason that people have sought refuge or moved is presumably oppression, war and unrest rooted in factors that include Sharia law. So you can't really blame people for asking the obvious question: Why in the world are they living here? There are plenty of countries you can move to that offer more than enough Sharia law, if that's what you desperately want.

Everyday values

Culture is a set of habits, and habits change over time. Our views on relationships, fashion, sports, music, language, etc are constantly changing. What was once considered shameful and taboo is now the norm; elsewhere, liberal secular values are being rolled back in favour of conservative religious values.

In the Western world, the compass is pointing in the direction of freedom. Liberation and freedom. Gone are the former constraints, be they conservative or religious. In this part of the Western world, it is now normal and fully acceptable to be homosexual. That wasn't the case 50 years ago. Putin's Russia is moving in the opposite direction, leading to the tragic persecution of homosexuals. In the spirit of the Renaissance, the Western world has slowly but surely taken life into its own hands and liberated us from a god-given, predestined world view. We can make a difference in this world; not all things are predetermined.

Religion has been relegated to the private sphere, rather than a dominant and guiding political force in society.

This struggle culminated in the 1960s. The extrication from the final remnants of patriarchal habits, gender roles, authorities and the right of young people to decide for themselves challenged established habits at the time, but virtually all of these things are now an integral part of our society.

We listen to rock music much more than chamber music. We wear jeans rather than suits. Our young people decide who they want to kiss – without asking their parents first. We have the right to an abortion. We strive for complete equality between the sexes. There is free access to pornography. And, as previously mentioned, we have succeeded in raising new generations who view homosexuals as a natural part of society.

The centre-left can jubilantly endorse all of these developments, for it has ushered in most of this progress. Things may appear grim to others. However, the majority of people can vouch for most aspects of the total package.

But one can genuinely doubt whether the majority of immigrant communities feel the same way.

A different view on gender equality is readily evident in many immigrant circles. The man and the boy typically enjoy a higher status than the woman and the girl. The family structure is often patriarchal, with the father as the dominant and decision-making figure. For matters big and small, he is the supreme authority. His honour and status in immigrant circles is based on how zealously he upholds this authority – thus paving the road to an unfathomable array of problems. This is no recipe for success in a secular Western world – on the contrary.

A mayor of a suburb to the west of Copenhagen once told me that this social control is virtually absolute and systematised. With the onset of menstruation, girls are considered a sex object by the men and must therefore cover their hair with a scarf and only allow it to hang uncovered in front of their closest family. And it goes further than just that. All former socialising with friends of both sexes is largely forbidden. Out of sight is out of social control, so these girls may no longer enjoy a film night at a girlfriend's house (other men and boys might be there too), and it's also a no to school camps and after school classes (unless it's sewing), while participation in various religious schools and programmes is compulsory.

Furthermore, the choice of marriage partner is still largely a matter determined by the family and patriarch. It is claimed that the young girl can say no, but it takes superhuman strength to resist such pressures. The number of immigrant girls who marry non-Muslims is barely measurable. This is not a matter of pure chance – it's a reflection of systematic oppression.

The amazing thing is that if ethnic Danish, Norwegian, German or Spanish girls had been subjected to similar treatment, we would have seen the intense and unwavering involvement of the centre-left, leftists, feminists, and anyone else affiliated with liberating views and ideals.

But when it comes to Muslim girls, the choir falls silent. Despite the fact that crisis centre upon crisis centre is filled with immigrant women who have suffered extreme abuse, and even though it is widely known and evident how scarves and marriages are imposed and observed, people keep any criticism to themselves. The most grotesque thing of all is that they do it in the name of goodness.

Any criticism of immigrants' habits and behaviour can be seen as doing the bidding of the right-wing, and therefore people keep their traps shut. At the same time, they are so critical of Western society's values that they pour adulation on the strong culture and family bond of these new citizens. It would really be quite comic if it weren't so tragic.

And the solution? It's right in front of us. The centre-left must simply stand by its views – and remain colour blind and proactive in the pursuit of its values.

This means speaking out publicly on behalf of the girls. This means that we should view the scarf in the 2010s like we viewed the bra in the 1970s. This means that somebody should protect and help the girls who resist their fathers' tyranny. This includes physical protection, as well as spiritual and intellectual support in our writing, speech, and everyday conduct. The freedoms stemming from the youth rebellion which are now enjoyed by many must also be brought to those who they haven't yet reached.

If successful, it will change immigration forever. When you give people the right to decide who they want to kiss and for how long, time will become our ally in integration. Or, if you will: Love will become the driving force for integration.

And the boys and their fathers? Things will also change for them. There's no longer any guarantee of having a spouse and a family. You have to behave politely, properly, courteously, and whatever else it takes to find love between two people. And no, the family patriarch does not have the right to control marriage, income, residence, religion and friendships.

Well goodbye then

And what if you don't want to live according to these ideals of freedom? What if you find the habits and values of the Middle East preferable?

The right thing must be to give the individual a choice: You can stay, if you want to integrate yourself and your family. If not, we will help you settle in another part of the world that is more conducive to your values.

This return (or repatriation) is of course possible, but it can also be difficult. The future may be uncertain in terms of income, health insurance, schooling, job opportunities, etc. In this regard, we must be helpful and develop schemes to ensure that families are reasonably comfortable with their decision to leave the West. Solutions could range from cash payments for settling in the new location and/or health insurance for a number of years. The important thing is that these schemes are genuine and comprehensive.

If they are, then the choice we give people is also fair. You and your family can choose to stay here and become a part of our common country and culture. Or you can live a life in a different society that is based on the values that suit you.

We must put an end to taking up residence in a Western society while being deeply opposed to that very society. It is not good for the individual, and it is not good for the society. The centre-left must be resolute in asking the individual to make a decision: Become a part of the society that integrates you, or leave that society and build a life somewhere else. This is not an unreasonable demand.

The willing

When a young girl of Kurdish origin who lives in Denmark stands out and does everything we ask of her, she is taking on an epic burden. Her insistence on freedom of personal choice in matters of love, marriage, residence, education, attire and recreational activities may be tantamount to severing ties with her family, friends and a sense of security in her life.

She – and the many others like her who openly embrace life in Denmark and the customs and rights entailed therein – deserves great admiration. And what's more – she also deserves whatever help and support we can offer.

When close family members become enemies, and old-fashioned matters of honour must be settled, it's not easy to be of non-Danish ethnic origin and to stand alone in defending the principles of personal freedom. It may even put one's life in danger. As a society, we must step up to protect and help these individuals – while sharing stories of those who choose this path and encouraging others to follow their example. Because this is the only path forward: enabling young people to liberate themselves from the constricting ties of family and culture.

And the young girls and young boys are out there – but they are also largely left to fend for themselves. The public debate must make it clear to them – and their parents – what is normal and reasonable in the Western world and tell them that they have the right to seize their freedom. It's startling how silent the traditional left wing has been in this debate, considering its values of feminism and the like. Whereas they avidly demonstrate and engage in activism for Metoo or the survival of marshland frogs, they're typically absent from the debate on the freedom of young immigrants.

And it's more than just the young people. It's the taxi driver who works long hours and does his best to fall in line and become integrated, and who does not subscribe to extreme beliefs and views. Or the industrial worker with roots in Pakistan who has been successfully employed for 30 years on the same job, and who proudly sees his children get an education and become a part of the future in Danish society.

At every turn throughout Denmark, you'll find small shops and industrious individuals with non-Danish ethnic backgrounds who are working hard to make ends meet, be it as a hairdresser, pizzeria owner, greengrocer, sign maker, bicycle retailer, baker, or highly educated financial broker. Their diligence and dedication is laudable. Work is, and will continue to be, an important element of a successful life and integration. But this alone is not enough for successful integration – your heart must also be in it.

Some generations ago, many Jews came to Denmark. They also faced difficulties while settling in Denmark and integrating, but they chose to integrate. They even had a strategy for this. They adopted Danish names and surnames, and slowly but surely they became intertwined in Danish society. And they're still there, some of whom still maintain their faith and customs without problems with the rest of society. This exemplary model should serve as inspiration for the new immigrants.

THE SLOWDOWN

The Western world is currently working to slow down a disaster. The number of refugees and immigrants from the Middle East/Islamic world is so great that it has actually caused a collapse in many communities.

For example, the number of refugees that came to Europe during the Syrian civil war caused even "humanistic" nations to resurrect their national borders. The Chancellor of Germany said "we'll manage it", but they couldn't. In Germany, France, the Netherlands and Sweden, the combination of new residents and those already living there who were having a hard time integrating ultimately put law, order and the welfare society on standby.

Core European countries are facing the prospect of Muslim majorities in local areas – and significant changes in the overall population composition – within the near future. For example, in a scenario with a high rate of immigration – i.e. the current scenario – Sweden will have a 30% Muslim population in 2050. We are facing a truly dramatic transformation of Europe.

In response to the refugee crisis in Europe, measures were successfully taken in 2015 to close off parts of the route taken by refugees and migrants, particularly those crossing through Turkish territory. These measures were successful due to an agreement with Erdogan and Turkey, and they will remain successful – until Erdogan changes his mind. In other words, we're in the pocket of a despot.

The same can be said of the refugee/migrant route crossing the Mediterranean, which passes through Libya. These measures are also dependent on agreements with local despots, and they're not even particularly successful at that.

A detailed analysis of the scope, composition and organisation of the migrant flow should have the European leftist elite in an uproar, as very few of them are actually refugees. The vast majority are economic migrants from a wide range of very different populations and countries. Common to them all is their exploitation by cynical human traffickers who charge them exorbitant sums. The share of women trafficked to Europe for prostitution and ruination is alarmingly high.

The business model of human traffickers involves them placing migrants in dilapidated boats and inflatable rafts, and then capsizing off the Libyan coast so that humanitarian organisations have to rescue the passengers into their own boats. This is grotesque and outrageous.

In the name of humanism, aid organisations organise and fund rescue boats, thus becoming an integral part of the human traffickers' business case. A major Danish left-wing newspaper, Politiken, even gave its "freedom award" to these aid organisations, emphasising that they were saving all those who politicians want to see drown. The nausea induced by that statement lingers to this day.

With their foot inside the EU, each of these asylum seekers gains access to a wide range of rights. Thus begins a protracted application process, and even if it ends with a rejection, many of these newcomers will stay nonetheless – either as illegal immigrants or by finding a new path to approval.

There are no two ways about it: those with the means are those who get a chance in Europe.

This traffic must be stopped – and not by our continuing to curb the civil rights of citizens of throughout Europe and the Western world. We simply must take control of who, and how many, are allowed into our countries. Otherwise it will soon be the end of these countries as we know them.

The solution is simple: If you enter the country by invitation, you will be escorted to a reception centre, where your case will be considered. If you are a refugee, you must be aided in refugee camps that provide shelter and protection.

Or, in other words: It's a "no go" for the business of human traffickers, and a "no go" for us being in the pocket of Erdogan. States and governments have the power to decide.

Is it feasible to establish one or more such centres? Yes, certainly. Just as there are also many refugee camps around the world, and much like Australia, which built a camp on an island. And yes, there must be proper conditions in the refugee camps to which people are transferred, with true protection, decent living conditions, schooling, etc.

Every Western country can thereby decide for itself how many new citizens and what types they want in the country.

Control over the number of migrants and control over national borders are the keys to convincing populations to once again entrust the centre-left with power.

Massive problems abound throughout Europe, where ghettos of Middle Eastern/Islamic immigrants live in parallel societies, where the country's language is not spoken and the country's culture is not lived. These mini-societies come from countries such as Turkey, as seen in connection with the Turkish vote to reform the constitution in a more conservative/Islamic direction, which garnered greater support among Turks living in European countries than in Turkey itself.

We must therefore take resolute action and set limits on how large a share of bilingual or difficult to integrate residents are allowed in a municipality and/or area. If this figure exceeds 30% it will be hard to distribute among different forms of housing, and day care institutions and schools will experience difficulties. So, 30% is likely a very good number. This would result in a huge redistribution of immigrants from Middle Eastern/Islamic backgrounds, but if we do not address the issue of housing, we cannot achieve optimum integration. This means that we are facing extensive demolition of ghetto housing complexes, strict management of housing waiting lists, and strict management of relocation to and from municipalities. Western society must get its housing policy and integration efforts in order; otherwise, we are permitting parallel societies and failed integration.

And assuming that the housing policy works, a gigantic task lies in store. Helping children who can't speak the language master it. Creating jobs for everyone in the family, including mum. Making sports clubs and local communities secure and free of crime. Making the French immigrant French and the German immigrant German, and allowing time to work for this cause. And all this on the principle that everyone who is willing can have a chance – those who are not can emigrate to another country.

Main points

✓ A country must only accept the number of refugees and immigrants that it can successfully integrate within a manageable period of time. The rest must be helped and supported elsewhere.

✓ Acknowledging that there is a difference between cultural spheres, and thereby who you let into the country, is a crucial premise and is closely linked with how many people can be successfully integrated.

✓ We must expect immigrants to observe the nation's laws, learn our language, embrace the values on which our democracy is built, and make their contribution to society and country. That you are loyal to your new home.

✓ The centre-left must stand by its views and values – and remain colour blind and proactive in the pursuit thereof. This includes physical protection, as well as spiritual and intellectual support – in our writing, speech, and everyday conduct – for the girls and women who are oppressed daily.

✓ The centre-left must present immigrants with the choice to stay here and become part of our common country and culture, or to live a life in a different society based on the values that suit them.

✓ We must take control of who, and how many, are allowed into our countries. The solution for this is reception centres in refugees' local regions. If you arrive in the country without an invitation, you will be escorted to one of these camps.

✓ Every Western country can thereby decide for itself how many new citizens and what types they want in the country.

✓ Western society must get its housing policy and integration efforts in order; otherwise, we are permitting parallel societies and failed integration.

THE DEMISE OF RESPECT

The Danish system is designed so that a 1-year increase in average life expectancy triggers a 1-year increase in retirement age. This means that most Danes have a long stay in the labour market. A child born in 2018 will likely not be eligible for retirement until she is 74 years old. This represents a significant increase in the time individuals spend in the labour market, but fortunately also a significantly higher average life expectancy.

But of course, this is the average. Not all people are the same. Social heritage has a clear impact on average life expectancy. The better the education, the longer the life expectancy. The harder the physical work, the lower the life expectancy.

Until just a few years ago, Danes had the option of paying to sign up for early retirement benefit, which would allow them to retire up to five years before the state pension age. For all practical purposes, this scheme is now abolished. The average stay in the labour market is now the same, whether you're an office manager, a mason or a bus driver.

But one would think it obvious that there's a difference between being a mason, who embarks on demanding physical work at the age of 17, and being an upper secondary school teacher, who gets started as a 28-year-old after completing his studies. Although students can be trying at times, it's not unreasonable to assume that a mason will experience more wear and tear in his working life. But the approach is equal for bakers, office managers and everyone else. The future will show whether it's realistic to expect that Viggo, born in 2018 and a mason from 2035, will be able to work until the year 2109.

The average life expectancy by profession correlates closely with the corresponding length of training. A long academic education is akin to long life expectancy. The life expectancy of an unskilled worker is significantly shorter. And, as a result, the average remaining life expectancy after retirement varies significantly. With the elimination of early retirement benefit, there will be major differences in how people of different professions live and experience life after retirement.

It is interesting and thought-provoking to take a look at who took the initiative to eliminate the aforementioned early retirement scheme. Not surprisingly, masons and butchers weren't leading the charge, but rather academics and their parties. And the amazing thing was that they did it in a triumphant tone, and that some of the champions of eliminating early retirement benefit otherwise labelled themselves as centre-left. Under axioms such as "we can easily work longer", "we're always learning new things", etc, 30-year-old academics paraded around with big smiles and celebrated the scrapping of the scheme. Economists at the heart of Denmark's central administration also joined in the festivities – it all looked so good in the spreadsheet.

In Germany, a social democratic government implemented Hartz-4 reforms, sending wages plummeting. The result was more jobs, but also many workers who couldn't get by on a single full-time job.

But it looked so good in the spreadsheet.

Under Denmark's former social democracy/social liberal government, the government's finance committee examined a proposal to allocate an additional DKK 300 million to the unemployment benefit system because so many people were maxing out their eligibility, despite reassurances that the opposite would be true. The committee voted against the proposal. The next item on the agenda was aquatic environment plans. These plans aimed to ensure good ecological conditions, i.e. increased insect density in measurements taken near streams and rivers. The committee allocated DKK 2 billion for this purpose.

One can rightly – and indignantly – ask: What in the world has happened to the centre-left's moral compass?

And the answer is that there is massive social, cultural and educational divide in society, with executives and metropolises slowly losing touch and respect.

Education is a heavy-handed separator that starts early and just grows exponentially throughout life. After primary schooling, there is one decisive cultural and social difference between the choice to enrol at upper secondary school or pursue vocational training. At upper secondary school, you are quarantined with others intent on further continuing their education after graduation. In vocational training, you are introduced to the adults' workplace and everything that entails. And there's a world of difference. In the past, there were barriers to getting an education and the share of students who attended upper secondary school was significantly lower; as a result, people maintained their friendships and relations across professions and studies – and a component of their continuing education was rooted in the workplace. This is no longer the case. An 18-year-old upper secondary student has few to zero acquaintances who are training for a career as a craftsman. And that trend continues throughout their youth, in their family lives and in their careers. Relations between different parts of society have become less and less common.

And slowly but surely, the social and cultural habits and issues experienced by the well-educated have become the norm for public debate and political reform – because they belong to the vociferous and powerful segment of the population. They don't end up knowing anybody whose life is different from their own. And so, it's not all that difficult to envision that you could get a new academic kick out of getting a new bachelor's degree at the age of 61 and extending your work life with something exciting and new. But it's obviously a little more difficult to envision what it's like to be a

61-year-old construction worker who has to be at work at 6:30 on a January morning to install concrete walls and rebar.

Herein lies the problem: We've lost respect for the contributions of others.

Because no matter how hard you try, there will always be jobs which are, and will continue to be, less interesting to take up – where the job is something you do because you're providing for yourself and your family, and take pride in doing so. In these cases, happiness lies not in time spent at work, but rather one's free time, and even better: the prospect of a day when you can sleep until late in the morning after having worked all your life. The latter is what got the triumphant academics in such a tizzy, and so they stole it from so many, while giving themselves even higher pay and privileges.

It should be simple for the centre-left throughout Europe to rediscover its connection and respect for the masses. All it needs to do is to be conscious of its ideology and its roots.

The exodus from rural to urban areas has continued unimpeded since the early days of the industrial revolution. But in recent decades, this migration has been accompanied by sweeping structural reforms. Guided by Richard Florida's homage to the superiority of the creative class, suburbs and rural areas have been drained of content in the name of metropolises and efficiency. By

50

this line of thought, there is no reason for investment in preserving provincial and rural institutions, since the genesis of all wealth is rooted in the big cities.

Educational institutions, hospitals, police departments and courthouses have been systematically centralised, and Denmark's municipal reform caused mergers and the formation of significantly bigger municipalities. The country is speckled with monuments to the municipalities of yore, towering empty in the landscape as citizens seek meaningful ways of putting them to use. The feeling of abandonment is palpable, while a critical examination of the administrative expediency of centralisation reveals questionable results. In the name of efficiency, local communities with decades upon decades of history have been ripped up by the root, leaving half-deserted small towns and suburbs behind in the rubble.

A rural town that may have previously been home to a population of 5,000 and a municipal council whose members were largely familiar to locals is now part of a municipality of 80,000 people, where most people barely know a single council member. The powerlessness is virtually all-encompassing. And the typical outcome is local stagnation and decline, with empty shops and ramshackle buildings lining the town streets. Market forces are the best hope for development, but they don't raise their head until all the assets are decimated.

Once again, respect is the keyword. If you aren't able to empathise and acknowledge that people who don't live right in the heart of the big city also want decent schools, decent nursing homes, shops that are open, and community institutions that are part of their daily lives, then you are further contributing to the mounting divide.

Nobody expects the people of a small town, or even a medium-sized city, to have the same facilities at hand as the big city, but it is reasonable to object to everything crumbling right before your eyes as the spreadsheet controllers of the big city are busy stressing the last institution out of town.

Can we afford the less than perfect?

A function of our efficient, industrious and skilled society is that some people can't cut it.

For some people, the challenges of existence amass to an unmanageable obstacle in daily life. These crises can be triggered by a death in the immediate family or a physical injury – or by a mind so plagued with demons that all control and joy in life evaporate. Or it could be that all the expectations and demands we impose on each other in our breakneck society just get to be too much, causing people to give up or collapse with stress and other illnesses.

Common to them all is that they count negatively in the spreadsheet.

It is expensive for society when a 35-year-old man suddenly can't attend to his job (as he otherwise did) and instead lies in bed staring at the ceiling for a year – and after three years of psychiatric counselling and various diagnoses, he still isn't healthy. Or the young upper secondary school student, who suddenly stops coming to school midway through her studies, losing the desire to learn, socialise and generally live, and who clearly needs help but can't find any.

The question is whether it is people's own fault, a matter of chance, or the fault of society that many people struggle with such massive personal problems that they are unable to successfully make their lives work.

The answer is that it's probably a combination of all these factors, but there's no denying that a large part of the population are afflicted by such tribulations to a greater or lesser degree.

And it is equally clear that help is not prescribed by the public system until the damage is significant and visible. To a great extent, people who suffer from social and mental problems are left to their own devices.

But the public sector probably shouldn't be the ones to solve this issue in its entirety. And swerving off the joyous and rambling path of life shouldn't automatically trigger a cavalry of public treatment providers. Rather, what is needed is people helping people, and institutions and workplaces that exhibit inclusive flexibility. But they're certainly not doing that today. On the contrary, jobs and schools are demanding ever greater productivity and efficiency. And that's all fine and good, but if there isn't room for people to fail, then the result will be far too many unhappy people.

Conversely, the answer isn't throwing rationality or prosperity to the wind and chasing the siren song of basic income and longing for the good old days – because there is no such thing as "good old days". There is a past where we were poorer, less effective and less organised, and it would puzzling to strive for a return to that state of affairs. Ultimately, it's a matter of distributing today's prosperity, which includes making room for those among us who fail – and that is a political choice.

Pretty much everybody knows that people are not perfect. But our current approach, which largely leaves people to deal with their issues in private, is untenable. Those planning society, businesses and work processes must also accept the responsibility of incorporating respect and room for the ranks of the non-perfect – because we are at the root of many of these problems, and because coming to people's aid in time and helping to prevent their problems from snowballing can be the most economically prudent decision we can make.

The gift of culture

For some people, life is a world of classical masterpieces, bookshelves, theatre, art and aesthetics from day one. This typically is closely linked with affluence, but not always. Having the privilege of an artistic and cultural head start in childhood is not to be envied, but as a society we must strive to give such blessings to a wider swathe of our population.

And that is why we structure and subsidise many of society's core cultural institutions. Orchestras, niche poetry, ballet and all kinds of museums are excluded from the logic of market economy and endowed with massive subsidies because society considers these activities valuable and worthy of preservation.

The biggest problem is not that society's elite flock to massively subsidised ballets and plays – subsidies paid for by all taxpayers. Rather, the problem is that this very audience tends to denigrate and downplay the importance of the cultural preferences among the rest of the population.

Because it's not the expenses for pop music, country music, line dancing, bingo, revues and Irish folk music that are weighing down the cultural budgets. There appears to be an unwritten rule that the more expensive it is, the less accessible it is for ordinary people. This goes for the price, physical distance and the prerequisite understanding required of the audience. The only thing certain to make it out to these people is the bill.

Decades of elitist art and cultural development have occurred without any particular involvement of the broad population – a fact that doesn't seem to bother those involved a smidgen.

The cultural elite of the big city can live in state-subsidised peace.

These circumstances can be leveraged to look down even more on cultural activities in the provinces, wrapping themselves in the bubble of their own milieu and orbiting completely out of touch with the lives and culture of the broad population. It is a contract shaped and dictated by one side and paid for by the other. Which begs the question: Is it a tenable contract for the future?

THE NEW ECONOMIC INEQUALITY

– countering the crusade of greed

For those who ascribe to the belief that the world is only progressing, there's bad news in store. Or rather, the world is certainly progressing economically, and we have grown richer and richer. Only those in favour of a just distribution of the wealth will find the news dismaying.

Since the start of the 1980s, the GDP of the United States has doubled. Meanwhile, the average household income for families has stagnated. Average real wages for the American middle class have essentially remained unchanged from 1972 to 2007. Productivity has doubled in that same period.

Looking to the 1% richest segment of the population, we find that they own 34% of the wealth in the United States. This same figure in Europe is 24%.

And what do these figures tell us? Well, the rich have stockpiled a colossal share of the wealth, and the masses must get by with less than before, little or nothing. A crusade of greed unleashed in the 1980s under the leadership of Thatcher and Reagan – and inspired by Friedman and the Chicago School – continues to the present day, as the world's richest people shamelessly and rabidly hoard as much as possible, with no regard and no restraint. And at the time of this writing, they have elected one of the more vulgar members of their ranks to lead the White House. How the right wing around the world can rejoice in this state of affairs is unfathomable – most of those who might consider voting for this wing will never even get close to benefiting from these developments. And for the people who, in the absence of legal protection and strong labour unions, are witnessing the decline of their prosperity and the rise of insecurity, it is quite simply heartless.

The new economic inequality, launched by Reagan and Thatcher, is one of the most important issues for the centre-left to address and offer alternatives that will reverse these trends.

It's really quite simple: Rich people must pay a fair tax.

Prevent the rise of a new nobility:
Impose an estate tax on large inheritances

And to begin with, let's just focus on the estate. If we keep reducing inheritance taxes, then we are permitting the rise of a new nobility over generations – a nobility that will wield significant economic and political dominance. This is an unacceptable scenario, and we should fight for a common tax floor to ensure fair inheritance taxation.

Picturesque and moving industrial tales abound,

stories of the entrepreneur who started in his garage and ended up with an automobile factory that brought jobs and prosperity. And we must respect these entrepreneurs greatly. But we can also express our distaste with the past efforts of Rockefeller and Vanderbilt to pull off a political coup of the United States to protect their own interests, or our disgust with the anything but sympathetic efforts of the Koch brothers to do the same in today's USA – or that Henry Ford had a photo of Hitler on his desk, or that the German automobile industry can get away with fraud because they have all the major political parties in its pockets. There is no reason for naivety. Wealthy individuals exercise political power to benefit their own interests – granting their heirs the right to carry on this tradition only makes things worse.

On the other hand, society has no interest in splitting up and destroying well-functioning companies due to taxation on the generational handover of an estate. This also applies in cases where there are many heirs. Therefore, the best thing we can do is to ensure that it is economical, legal and tax-efficient to establish private commercial foundations that are governed by standard law. The company can thereby continue operations under the management of a foundation and professional executive management – while cash transfers to heirs must be executed by other means.

Progressive income tax

If you are amongst those with the highest salaries,

then you also pay proportionately more in tax – this is known as progressive taxation. Top-bracket tax and progressive taxation according to income is a fine principle, as it gives those with the lowest salaries a tax advantage and thereby seems to be an equalising expression of solidarity. This form of taxation is under attack, and over the last 30 years it has been significantly curtailed.

There are major differences from country to country in terms of tax brackets, how many people are in each bracket and how high the taxes are. If too many ordinary wage earners find themselves in the top bracket, then the system becomes too rigid. A complete abolishment will lead to more injustice.

One good way of structuring this would be to decide that a fixed percentage of the highest incomes in society must always pay top-bracket taxation. The establishment of such a principle would be very easy to calibrate from year to year by the tax authorities. The level of this taxation can be determined according to political inclination.

Fair taxation is also a matter of taxing gains – be it capital gains from securities, or the profits from a car factory. This area of taxation is also witness to a grotesque competition where entire countries abandon everything in hopes of attracting the headquarters of international corporations. For example, the corporation tax rate in Ireland is 0% – so it comes as little surprise that they've had a bit of success in attracting international corporations. Thus begins an unseemly race to the bottom, where one country after the other succumbs to pressures to reduce its corporation tax – and cowing to the threats of companies that a failure to do so will cause them to desert the country. And if you think that this race ends in a big round zero, you can think again – they can even get subsidies, so you better believe that this goes into the planning process behind boardroom doors.

This trend must be stopped. From free trade zone to free trade zone. The European Union has successfully adopted a floor and a ceiling on VAT. The same must be done for corporation taxes. A solidarity pact should be established, by which all taxes except for income taxes are subject to a floor and a ceiling.

The message is really very simple: We'll give you free trade, but we demand the funding of welfare that can protect our lives.

WAGES

In 2016, the CEO of Walmart in the United States received a total salary of $236 million for the inconvenience. The head of Apple (those guys who can't be bothered with paying tax) had to make do with a paltry $150 million.

These grotesquely huge salaries – despite the fact that they almost certainly work hard and do a good job – stand out like a sore thumb in comparison to the incomes of other wage earners. And all throughout the

Western world, executive boards are awarding themselves astronomical salaries, and even more grotesque options. The latter is the big lottery ticket, with the only difference being that real lottery tickets don't pay off – these do.

In the same companies that ask for ever greater productivity from their employees, ever more flexible working conditions and, in the case of some countries, with stagnant or declining wages, they're holding a party for themselves on the executive floor, without restraint or self-control. There are countless examples, the most comedic of which is when a board chairman explains himself by saying that competitive reasons dictate that the company simply must pay a CEO hundreds of millions every year, or otherwise they won't be able to find a qualified candidate for the job.

Salaries and options have spiralled out of control. The boards are unable to do anything to stop it, or else they are co-conspirators. Something else is needed, and the right tool in this case is mandatory CSR – Corporate Social Responsibility – certification of companies.

We all know the concept of child labour – we don't want children to be harvesting coffee beans in the fields, we want them learning at school. Therefore, in most places you have the option of purchasing fair trade coffee. Consumers have to power to vote with their wallets, so to say, and it works!

Could the same be done in relation to CEO salaries? It can, and a standard for doing this could take many forms. For example, you could adopt rules that options must not comprise more than 20% of the total pay, that the total pay must not be more than 20 times the average salary of all company employees, or institute a fixed salary ceiling of $10 million.

This type of certification could provide a basis for consumer decisions on whether to invest in a company. And here, consumer does not mean those who shop in a supermarket – it means those who shop in the financial supermarket. All around the world, enormous fortunes are tied up in pension savings and transactions by nations and public sectors. In this arena, political decision makers or policyholders can adopt a policy of only investing in stocks and doing trade with companies who have a certain certification of their pay policy.

Denmark's GDP is 1.8 trillion DKK. Total pension savings in Denmark amount to more than 3 trillion DKK. Ordinary wage earners just have to agree that the allocation of THEIR money must not go to companies whose boards and executives cannot rein in their greed. The biggest obstacle to this may actually be the executives in control of these pension funds, but it's a great place to start.

But won't composite financial products, derivatives, just make it difficult to identify how companies interact, how products are structured, and how much is transferred from one place to the other, etc?

Yes, it is certainly complicated. But where there is a will, there is a way: not least because companies need investments and the extensive capital made available to them by wage earners and states. And with today's effective digital solutions, tracking the origin of any type of capital, service or product is possible and easy.

TAX EVASION

A favourite pastime of the particularly wealthy is to avoid paying taxes. They have no desire to contribute to the very same society that has made them wealthy by providing a welfare society and citizens who can purchase their goods. Extensive and persistent efforts are being made to channel money to tax havens, eagerly abetted by lawyers, auditors and the financial industry.

Over the past 20 years, bodies such as the OECD have sought to reach voluntary agreements with countries on measures to prevent tax fraud; despite reports of progress, periodic leaks reveal how fortunes are nonetheless being tucked away in Switzerland, Panama, the Cayman Islands, or wherever else possible.

The scope of this evasion is enormous. An estimated $6 trillion dollars is deposited in tax havens, and EU countries lose out on more than $1 trillion in tax revenue annually .

What's going on is disheartening – only surpassed by the fact that so little is being done to combat it.

While ordinary people pay tax – and, in some places, high taxes at that – there is a playground for the richest of the rich, where tax authorities are robbed of the ammunition to do something about it.

Something has to change.

The world – not least the global monetary world – is electronically intertwined. It isn't possible to carry out systematic, large-scale tax evasion without the aid of professional forces. And all of this can be traced.

Every lawyer, auditor, financial advisor or other person who contributes to facilitating tax evasion must face a fine, revocation of their licence to practice, and barring from any activity within the given trade area.

Every company with a branch or subsidiary in a tax haven must be subject to special tax audits – at their own expense – to provide certainty that they are not using transfer pricing schemes or tax planning to channel funds to these tax havens.

The trade area, e.g. the European Union, must commence negotiations with every suspected tax haven; in the absence of an agreement that provides transparency, they will be added to the list of tax havens. This also applies to nice, old, cosy nations such as Luxembourg, Switzerland and Gibraltar – we're done with their nonsense. If we are going to do business together, then the rules of the game must be enforced in full.

All around the world, Reagan and Thatcher are hailed within right-wing circles as noble role models for conservatism, and statues are even erected in their honour. Instead, monuments of shame should be erected, accompanied by information about how a few years of political power was used to demolish a century of progress, and how the world has become a worse, less secure and less just place because of the devastation invoked by them and their cronies. The new economic inequality stems from their era, and correcting their misdeeds is one of the centre-left's most pressing projects.

MAIN POINTS

✓ The new economic inequality, launched by Reagan and Thatcher, is one of the most important issues for the centre-left to address and offer alternatives to reverse these trends. Rich people must once again pay a fair tax.

✓ We do not want a new nobility – therefore, we must have a fair inheritance tax, and ensure that it is economically, legally and tax-efficient to establish private commercial foundations that are subject to standard law.

✓ Progressive taxation must be maintained. The broadest shoulders must bear the greatest burden, with one potentially useful principle being that a fixed percentage of the highest incomes in society must always pay top-bracket taxation.

✓ We want a solidarity pact from free trade area to free trade area, establishing a floor and a ceiling for corporation tax and other taxes.

✓ Salaries and options for executives and board members have spiralled out of control. We must institute CSR rules establishing that options must not comprise more than 20% of the total pay, and that the CEO's total pay must not be more than 50 times the average salary in the company, not to exceed a fixed ceiling of $10 million.

✓ Every lawyer, auditor, financial advisor or other person who contributes to facilitating tax evasion must face a fine, revocation of their licence to practice, and barring from any activity within the given trade area.

✓ Every company with branches or subsidiaries in a tax haven must be subject to special tax audits – at their own expense – to provide certainty that they are not using transfer pricing schemes or tax planning to channel funds to these tax havens.

THE CENTRE-LEFT'S PARTNERSHIP WITH THE BUSINESS COMMUNITY

The sources of prosperity

The story of a man who comes up with an idea. Works on it. Goes out to the garage and builds models. Starts up small-scale operations at a workshop and ends up with a huge factory, which generations later still stands proud in the landscape, generating wealth for shareholders and country. It's a good story, a true story, and a not unusual story.

From country to country, companies have grown and blossomed throughout the industrial age, powered by the industriousness of entrepreneurs and abetted by the requisite demand.

Our welfare in the modern Western world is built on the foundation of industry. The value of that produced by industry has lifted the population from a poor to a rich society – that is, of course, because there has also been a fair distribution of this wealth through wages and taxation.

And fortunately, the population has grown significantly since the dawning of industry, accompanied by an ever-growing array of new products and services. Attending a pitch event, where new entrepreneurs try to sell their ideas to investors, is a study in creativity and energy that delights and feeds a belief in progress.

Free competition in a free and accessible market – with tens of thousands of creative entrepreneurs and extremely skilled business leaders – is the breeding ground for the prosperity of the future. This competition and this market are the best friends and allies of the centre-left.

And the feeling is mutual.

In the everyday world of business, virtually all aspects of society are interwoven and cannot succeed without cooperation. If fire safety legislation hinders the construction of a new manufacturing unit, the company must get in contact with the decision makers. If there is a lack of qualified labour, it is too late to announce vacancies on the day the problem arises, because it takes years to educate young people. And it's not particularly expedient to have poorly functioning public transport, because that prevents a lot of people from getting to work on time.

A society and its businesses are closely connected. A well-functioning public sector with education, continued training, childcare, good roads and flexible bureaucracy is absolutely vital to the competitiveness of companies.

For many years, it was fashionable to relocate industry based in the old Western countries to more exotic regions, where the wages were certainly lower. But the lesson learned is that it takes more than that to ensure success. Competitiveness is about more than wage dumping; it is also a matter of the facilities of the surrounding society and the choices made by individual employees. In regard to the latter, the ever-growing automation and digitisation of production means that the demand for labour is not just a search for sweaty manual labourers, but for individuals who can think their way to designing and realising productive progress. These people are hard to find if they live in a country where they can barely survive on the low wages, with no social safety net, poor access to education and only the health insurance they can pay for themselves.

The future of manufacturing will require completely different employees than those Henry Ford plugged into the assembly line. It takes secure, highly trained and well-paid employees – an easy-to-embrace combination for the centre-left. The future of manufacturing will also be energy-intensive, which means energy will be a competitive parameter alongside wages. This parameter can be secured through green electricity and storage.

There will certainly be some people out there who can't control themselves, people who get warm and fuzzy at the thought of having children in Bangladesh sew our clothes for wages that barely provide the minimum needed for survival. But we'll have to take care of that by other means.

And then there's the fact that businesses, organisations and working methods are being challenged by the digital world. When an 18-year-old confusedly asks what a CD is, then you know things have changed quickly. Telling young people today that there was a time when you couldn't stream 24 million songs on your iPhone at any time and that you had to buy your CDs doesn't spark much interest on their part. They're past that point, and they're happy consumers of the new options. But let's stop for a minute. How is it that the big IT companies succeeded in offering so much music at such a low price? Because the payments to the individual artists have declined drastically. For one thing, the volume of music consumption obviously increases when so many people can gain access so cheaply, but the reasonable income once generated by a modest hit is now next to nothing.

It's certainly great for the 18-year-olds that they can hear a lot of music very cheaply, and it's great for the IT company that they can make a bunch of money by selling it, but is it fair to the artists?

When new platforms challenge old ways of working, thus creating progress and productivity, it's good for most people. But there is also reason to maintain that this progress shouldn't be pursued at all costs. Competition must be on fair terms. These terms include that taxes must be paid equally, that the country's laws must be observed, and that payment must be provided in accordance with the current conditions, which is understood as payment that enables individuals to provide for themselves and their families with a full-time job.

Given that this is fortunately possible, new inventions and progress will be the successful companion of the centre-left if we design our policies for such aims.

A classic right-wing angle would be to say that the health and well-being of companies are determined by competition in the market, and that politicians must solely focus on improving the conditions for doing business.

A classic left-wing angle was based on a labour struggle between shareholders and workers.

The latter of these battles, assuming the existence of a fair deal on proper pay and working conditions, is over. Instead, the centre-left sees convergent interests.

The company is interested in growth and progress. The employees have a clear interest in keeping the company in the country and gaining a share of the progress. Society and the state are interested in the company creating jobs and revenue for the country.

The state and society can thus benefit by pursuing a proactive business policy with the participation of all stakeholders. And this means that the state accepts the task of identifying the winners and cooperating with them.

In reality, it's not particularly leftist. A virtually uninhabitable, mosquito-infested swamp just 60 years ago, Singapore became one of the world's wealthiest nations through outstanding leadership and very active government involvement in business development. (However, not everything in the process was democratic and exemplary.) This was the conceptual model for the Danish "S-SF-R" (Social Democracy, the Socialist People's Party and the Social Liberal Party) government, which in 2013 launched a business policy that identified Denmark's positions of strength and initiated a dialogue with the business community and other stakeholders on ways of strengthening and improving the conditions for doing business.

The focus in each category, which included maritime blue Denmark, Danish design and Danish foods, was on existing commercial successes, followed by efforts to improve the conditions for continued and amplified success.

A broad range of participants were appointed to committees within each category and tasked with proposing improvements – on the condition that they must not be cost-intensive. These committees typically presented 40 to 50 recommendations on everything from de-bureaucratisation and restructuring of educational programmes, to new standards, etc. In this process, the government made two commitments: accepting an "adopt or explain" principle, by which it had to implement the proposals or provide an explanation for not doing so, and agreeing to a date at which it would be assessed on its implementation of the proposals – a public assessment available to all.

At the time of this writing, the second round of these business action catalogues is drawing to a close, and virtually all of those involved have expressed a desire to continue efforts within this framework.

Great strides can be taken when everyone cooperates with a business focus. The fact is that others never had this focus in the past. It can only be achieved by concentrating our abilities and efforts – this is precisely how Lee Kuan Yew created the world's greatest commercial success, and precisely how an old economy like Denmark has achieved new successes.

And nothing stands in the way of other countries adopting this same concept. No country will end up having everything for itself; the greater the production, the greater the trade and the greater the prosperity.

Where and why should the state operate businesses?

Public ownership of companies has taken many forms throughout the history of the Western world's nations. At one extreme, communism in Eastern Europe set new lows in state-owned inefficiency, and at the other you have an absolute minimum of public ownership, as seen in the US for instance.

The clear-cut lesson is that if the state-owned company does not bring in private capital and co-ownership in time, it tends to get bogged down in inefficiency.

Conversely, there are good reasons for the public sector to take the lead in forming companies in many areas. This applies in the case of natural public monopolies, as well as when there is a political desire to achieve a goal in which the market either cannot or will not invest.

It is sensible for us to agree that there should only be one grid for electricity, which makes it a natural public monopoly. It also seems reasonable that we only have one sewage system. And only one water supply system. And it also seems logical to stop at one network of railways. And one network of motorways and bridges, etc.

All of these are natural public monopolies, which

if thrown in the hands of private ownership could be exploited as a private monopoly. In this respect, the centre-left must stand firm – no crazy privatisation, aka Thatcher and Reagan, which leads to private monopolies, duopolies or other unhealthy market situations.

The picture gets a little more muddied when we progress further down this line of thought. From ancient times, the king and thereby the state established the postal service – since nobody else could – and the vast majority of nations are still involved in the ownership of these postal services. Whether continued ownership remains necessary in the midst of a digital age, with full-fledged competitors in the market, is now a good question.

Once upon a time, there were also state-owned bus companies in Denmark, and nobody really misses them. Or a clothing factory that was once used to sew uniforms. We can easily leave that to the market to figure out.

But these companies typically arose because there were no private sector players who could or would meet the need. And in these cases, it is both good and sensible for the state to take the lead.

A good example of a political desire being realised through state ownership and subsidisation is the green transition. In the 1980s, most people realised that global warming constitutes a serious problem. They understood that continuing to emit carbon at the same levels would drastically impact the Earth, with disastrous consequences for many people.

There was a political desire in Denmark to identify and develop non-nuclear alternatives to fossil fuels. One of the technologies selected for these efforts was wind turbines. At the start of this journey, wind turbines were not particularly efficient – in fact, they were decidedly inefficient. Only through major subsidies did the first generations of turbines see the light of day. But with continued political and financial support for wind energy efforts, the business case continued to improve year by year – because the technology continues to improve, and because the wind turbine manufacturers can invest in research and development with a reasonable certainty that there will be customers at the end of this road. The founding of DONG (now Ørsted) was part of these efforts – a 100% state-owned company whose responsibilities included the development of wind energy.

Seven generations of wind turbines later, wind turbines and related industry represents one of Denmark's biggest export businesses. Parts of DONG (Ørsted) have been divested along the way, and the value of the remaining 51% of shares has risen to more than 50 billion Danish kroner. Denmark's electrical supply can now be provided almost entirely by wind turbines. This significant political and economic progress was only made possible because the state took the lead, providing capital and covering risk throughout the first challenging decades.

The accumulated value of DONG/Ørsted can perhaps be used for new green investments.

It's time to set new goals, and let's stay in the green lane:

Regardless of the installation of a peculiar fellow in the White House, the incontrovertible fact is that we face a serious challenge with regard to our climate. Far too much fossil fuel is still being burned, we have problems with clean drinking water all around the world, and we have problems producing enough food on a sustainable basis like we do in Denmark.

The centre-left wants to solve these political issues. The market (and Trump) will not save us without some help. If we're talking about the development of technologies and production facilities with a timeframe of more than a decade, it will be difficult to find investors for these endeavours. But it is absolutely imperative that something is done.

Therefore, the right thing to do is for states to get involved, providing capital, responsibility and access to markets for ongoing development.

This goes for the development of green energy sources – a field where we have no idea what the best option will be in 40 years, but also a field in which we must invest now to ensure that our children and grandchildren will have good options to choose from. Perhaps it will be the well-known sources such as solar and wind – or they may be completely out of the picture in 25 years. But we will only find out by providing the means to develop new technologies.

And, importantly, we must crack the code when it comes to storing energy from green sources. In

Denmark, we can supply the country with 100% green electricity, but some days aren't very windy (fortunately), in which case we must use fossil fuels. And there are days when we produce more green electricity than we can use, and it goes to waste. Just think if we could store this energy – be it from wind or solar – and thereby ensure security of supply. We have no idea whether this will be done through the use of hydrogen, hot water or battery technology. We only know that we must commit to helping the first generations get up and running so that they can be developed commercially – and that this will take decades.

We must also develop new technologies and methods to produce more food.

In 2023, the population of Africa is expected to be larger than that of China and India combined, and in 2023, China, India and Africa will be home to more than half of the world's population. Or to make things even more interesting: how are we going to feed 9 billion people in 2050? We are already facing the prospect of demand outpacing the supply of food within 10 years' time.

A complex set of activities must be launched to prevent an epic disaster. One of the key challenges will be finding a way to produce more and better foods without causing an ecological catastrophe.

The story is basically the same for clean drinking water.

These are gargantuan tasks, but they are doable. The

alternatives are that we fight for the scarce existing resources, or transform existing states into hippie societies, neither of which seems particularly attractive.

MAIN POINTS

✓ Free competition in a free and accessible market
  – with tens of thousands of creative entrepreneurs
  and extremely skilled business leaders – is the
  breeding ground for the prosperity of the future.
  This competition and this market are the best
  friends and allies of the centre-left.

✓ A society and its businesses are closely connected.
  A well-functioning public sector with education,
  continued training, childcare, good roads and
  flexible bureaucracy is absolutely vital to the competitiveness of companies.

✓ When new platforms challenge old ways of working, thus creating progress and productivity, it's
  good for most people. But there is also reason to
  maintain that this progress shouldn't be pursued
  at all costs. Competition must be on fair terms.
  These terms include that taxes must be paid equally,
  that the country's laws must be observed, and that
  payment must be provided in accordance with the
  current conditions, which is understood as payment
  that enables individuals to provide for themselves
  and their families with a full-time job.

✓ The state must play a part in identifying the winners and executing proactive business policy in collaboration with all stakeholders.

✓ If natural public monopolies are thrown in the hands of private ownership, they could be exploited as a private monopoly. In this respect, the centre-left must stand firm – no crazy privatisation, aka Thatcher and Reagan, which leads to private monopolies.

✓ Sometimes the state must take charge and operate a business if the market cannot handle the task. Therefore, the right thing to do is for states to get involved, providing capital, responsibility and access to markets for the overall development of society.

✓ The state must embrace a long-term, shared responsibility and proactively engage in solving the world's challenges, for example renewable energy, storage of renewable energy, clean drinking water and the production of tomorrow's foods.

TWO EXPRESSWAYS TO FREEDOM: EDUCATION AND HEALTH

If you visit London and Copenhagen, there are plenty of entertaining and interesting things to fill your time with. But should you find yourself bored nonetheless, try taking a look at the plumbing work. Or the masonry work. Or the painting work. My experience and claim is that you'll discover a world of difference in the quality. Plumbing work in London often looks like it was done by somebody with 10 thumbs. This isn't intended to unnecessarily offend the Brits, and there is almost certainly very fine craftsmanship to be found in Buckingham Palace, but that's something the author of this book hasn't yet had the opportunity to verify. Rather, it is meant to illustrate a point. Education is not just education. If the quality is absent, education can prove to be an exercise in futility.

In Denmark, we go to great lengths to uphold and ensure proper craftsmanship. We train young people for four years to become plumbers, masons, painters, etc – and we ensure that they all acquire sufficient knowledge of the basic skills needed.

In other countries, the feeling is that this can be done in record time, or that people are just born for the job and don't need any schooling.

We also educate the nursery teachers who care for

our children. They are equipped with skills and knowledge relating to teaching, learning, children's signals, socialising, and playing with young children, giving them the best possible start in life. Caring for children is not just a matter of keeping an eye on them; it is a profession requiring skills and abilities.

The constant and unquenchable thirst of right wing governments in Denmark to cut back on vocational education programmes is a plague that requires our unwavering resistance.

The welder working at Danfoss almost never gets dirty in the course of a workday. LEAN, digitisation, teamwork and continuing education have ensured that the company's ever-increasingly automated industrial production is based in Denmark, and for six years in a row they have achieved annual productivity improvements of more than 10%.

Nearly 60% of Danish youth pursue higher education, attending university is free, and you even get a 6,500 kroner monthly stipend from the state during your five-year study.

All around the world, competent young people struggle for the opportunity to get an education, and their parents must often abandon all hope of being able to pay for their children's studies.

The number of unskilled workers continues to decline, but there is still much progress left to be made. On the other hand, many unskilled workers are equipped with some skills or partial training that ensures a high level of professionalism.

Education is the foundation for Denmark's high employment, our low unemployment, our efficient production, our high quality craftsmanship, our strong competitiveness and our high level of service.

And nonetheless, this sector is under constant attack. It is as if the right wing feel physically ill at the thought of their children having to share an education with all the rest of us. And therefore, they want differences, built on fees and user payments.

The pattern is also clear around the globe: As soon as you establish major payment barriers in the form of student tuition at universities and a lack of income in the form of state stipends, you exclude a large share of young people from getting an education, and those affected are all on the same side of the socioeconomic divide.

Instead, the ambition should be focused on finding even more effective ways of breaking with social heritage. It's still the case that children from the lower social classes have a difficult time coping with university studies. And, as mentioned, the treatment of vocational programmes like an unloved stepchild has caused the share of young people trained in a craft to decline and stagnate; thankfully, however, the quality of this craftsmanship has remained intact.

And there are certainly many aspects of the educational system worthy of reform; the length of studies, more flexible partial training and the conditions of student life are all topics to be discussed for the sake of improving productivity in the education world.

Meanwhile, the new technologies may bring about the greatest educational advance in history – if we are able to manage them wisely and properly.

Digitisation of learning environments, such as adaptive programs to give dyslexic and reading-challenged children the tools to succeed on an equal footing with classmates; adaptive mathematical programs that ensure individual progression; automatic language translation, etc. The barriers of yesterday are being cleared from our path at breakneck speed, and there is good reason to applaud what we are witnessing.

Decades from now, it may be pure nonsense to talk of limiting access to universities. A digitised classroom, with digital lectures and teaching, and digital exams – why even show up for class in person, unless you have a laboratory to attend to? In principle, won't it be fully possible to complete university studies in economics at a university in Ontario without having ever set foot on its campus?

And if we equip a street child in India with an iPad, a charger and a login to an educational programme, are there any limits to who and how many we give the opportunity?

And if, suddenly, the 300,000 Danes and millions of others around the world with dyslexia no longer have to deal with his challenge because all devices take this into account, then who knows what great untapped resources can be unleashed?

Politicians must of course generally refrain from predicting what the brave new world of technology holds. More often than not, the future outcome is retrospective mockery. But the above is just the tip of the iceberg. Technology offers an amazing opportunity to reduce costs, while expanding and democratising education to an unprecedented extent.

We in the centre-left must be ready. With our principles of free and equal access, where proposed barriers, such as tuition and the elimination of student grants, must be combated before the right wing ever manages to institute them.

If the centre-left embraces the brave new world, then the centre-left will truly become a progressive movement.

Without free access to education and decent living conditions for students, there is no true freedom for the individual – and that, of course, is one of the centre-left's signature projects.

HEALTH

When confronted with somebody who is ill, a normal human reaction is to wish them a full recovery. And you probably also hope that you never have to face a serious illness yourself, but rather can live to your last day as a healthy and agile 98-year-old.

Unfortunately, that's not the way things go for the

majority of the population. It may well be that science can solve this problem for us, but until then we must accept that people will become ill and can die from serious diseases.

One-third of the population will be diagnosed with cancer in their lifetime. The fear and anxiety such a diagnosis instils in patients and their families leaves no doubt in their hearts as to whether it makes sense to pay for and invest in cancer treatment. The same should also be true of those whose lives are not directly impacted. Could you imagine having to tell two 10-year-old boys with the same cancer diagnosis, and their families, that one will receive the best treatment available, and the other will not?

Doesn't sound nice, does it? But that's what we are doing if we accept private insurance. When we put free and equal access to health on standby, we differentiate, and the result is crystal clear: Those adversely affected are those with the fewest economic means. There is no "but" and no exceptions to the rule – that's precisely what happens. The right wing employs lies and deceit on this matter, apparently because they are so driven to ensure good treatment for themselves, or based on some twisted form of trickle-down reasoning that if things are going well at the top, then it will generously drip down to those below. And that's bullshit – every iota of it.

Private practices or, for that matter, private hospitals is not the issue – a little competition is fine, especially if it is fair competition. The crucial factor is free and equal access to the best possible treatment.

The purpose of private insurance is to make a difference. It enables you to jump the queue, opt for somewhat better preventive examinations, a little more physiotherapy and subsidies for various drugs.

The smaller the scope of this insurance, the better, but it certainly is not good.

The right wing is fighting hard around the world to increase the amount of private insurance, and if we don't make sure that we curb its spread, it will slowly but surely undermine the universal health care system. The recipe of right wing governments is to cut health spending and offer tax allowances and other privileges for private insurance.

If we win the battle for free and equal access to health and a publicly-financed universal health care system, we can claim to have the foundation for a welfare society. If we lose, support for the welfare society – and its functionality – will be eroded.

Health is expensive, but the most expensive health is through private solutions. While Denmark spends 10.9% of its GDP on health care for all of its citizens, the United States spends 17.1% of its GDP to provide health care for only a portion of the population. Life expectancy in Denmark is 81 years, while in the United States it is 79 years.

The way we structure our health service and the way we prioritise new procedures and new drugs is difficult and full of dilemmas, but there are no arguments for leaving these matters to the market. However, there is no doubt that we can manage organisation of the health sector better (see the section of this book on that topic).

One of the best examples of the consequences of a predominantly market-based and user-paid system is dental treatment. Children in Denmark have full dental coverage until the end of municipal primary and lower secondary school, after which the tasks of finding and paying the significant costs of dental treatment become a private matter.

And what do young people do with their limited means? Well, they essentially never go to the dentist – or, at least, not until much later in life, often long past the point of irreversible damage to their teeth. Once again, these detrimental impacts are reserved for those in the lower income brackets. The worse your socioeconomic standing, the less you visit the dentist, and the bigger the problems you will encounter later in life. So when you're 55 years old and can't pay for a new set of dentures, forcing you to try your hand at exotic trips to Romanian dentists or the like, you've got a recipe for misery.

The above example is limited to dentists. But it could just as well be other ailments where people are subjected to these barriers and user payment. If you think that all people, regardless of income, have a right to decent dental treatment, the current state of affairs is a sad one.

Inequality in the brave new world

Optimistic news reports on advances in medical procedures and drug treatment reveal that we will live increasingly longer lives. And there is every reason to take joy in this development – if, that is, it occurs on acceptable conditions. Very few of us want to end life in a dysfunctional state, be it physical or mental.

Over the past 100 years, life expectancy has skyrocketed. In Denmark, we now live to an average age of 81 years, and all signs indicate that this number will continue to rise. And to boot, it doesn't appear that we will spend this additional time on Earth being sick. The pattern of disease is the same, with the last couple of years often being very care-intensive.

There are reports of impending medical breakthroughs to combat cancer, HIV vaccines, weight-loss drugs that actually work and can reduce cases of severe obesity, diagnosis based on a single drop of blood taken in the comfort of your home, drugs to prevent dementia, and stem cells that can produce replacement parts for the body.

All these things are fantastic, and the centre-left must embrace it all, while also rectifying another injustice. Dental treatment is not the only thing that's wrong when we take a look at the socioeconomic landscape.

The average life expectancy in Denmark of unskilled workers is 11 years lower than for academics. The incidence of lifestyle disease is far higher among the most disadvantaged. Yes, this is because they live less healthy and have more strenuous jobs. And no, it's not just the individual's fault. The food you eat, the sweets you eat, and the alcohol and tobacco culture from your childhood all follow you into adulthood. It's just as difficult to break with this heritage as in the case of education. And once you are obese at a young age, it becomes a lifelong battle to keep the weight off. Kilos and calories pile up because the junk food eaten is often cheaper than healthy food – and much of the food industry has filled its products with salt, sugar and quick carbohydrates so that people get hungry again faster, which means they can make more money. And thus, we see a large increase in the number of obese children.

THE BEST WAY IS THE TAX WAY

A Danish millionaire – one of those with enough money at a young age to live the rest of life without a care – moved to the United States with his wife and children. A trip to the emergency department at an American hospital cost more than two thousand dollars for 20 minutes of treatment. But he had insurance that covered the cost. In Denmark, you never even see a bill for A&E treatment, for hospitalisation or for operations, and there's a cap on how much you have to pay for medicine. For nurseries and day care, parents pay no more than one-third of the cost; the rest is funded by the public sector. It is free to attend municipal primary and lower secondary school and upper secondary school, and to pursue vocational education. Young people receive a state education grant for up to six years of study – and it never has to be paid back. Young students are eligible for housing subsidies. If you lose your job, you can claim unemployment benefit for up to two years if you are a member of an unemployment insurance fund.

When you turn 67, you receive a state pension for the rest of your life, regardless of your previous income.

The total tax burden in Denmark is 45.9%. In the United States, it is 26%.

So what did the bottom line show for our Danish millionaire? Well, once he had paid for all his American insurance coverage, it was cheaper to live in Denmark.

The bottom line is only less favourable for the super-rich. For all the rest of the population, it is a good idea – both financially and for the sake of personal freedom. Whether or not some of this free and equal access and tax-funded solidarity is delivered through the private sector is immaterial – the important thing is that the individual has a right to freedom, and this is only possible through tax-funded solidarity. Insurance is the path to inequality and a loss of freedom.

MAIN POINTS

✓ Education is not just education. If the quality is absent, it can all prove to be an exercise in futility.

✓ Education is a prerequisite for high employment, low unemployment, efficient production, expert craftsmanship, strong competitiveness and a high level of service.

✓ Payment barriers – in the form of student tuition at universities and a lack of income from state stipends – exclude a large share of young people around the world from getting an education, and those affected are all on the same side of the socio-economic divide.

✓ Digitisation of education can eliminate the barriers of the past and offer access and freedom of education to those who would otherwise never have it. The centre-left must embrace and encourage these advances.

✓ If you put free and equal access to health on standby, you differentiate, and the result is crystal clear: Those adversely affected are those with the fewest economic means.

✓ Private practices or, for that matter, private hospitals is not the issue. The crucial issue is free and equal access to the best possible treatment.

✓ The best foundation for free and equal access for all citizens is tax-funded welfare on the principle of solidarity, without insurance and high user fees.

THE PUBLIC SECTOR

Budget control and autonomy

MANAGING THE PUBLIC SECTOR

The public sector is a cornerstone of the welfare society. Through the public sector, we have successfully "built a building that shields us from want", in the form of a social safety net, free and equal access to good health, access to education and the right to compassionate care, whether you are a child or an elderly person who needs help with the daily chores of life.

The welfare society and its building – the public sector – have been the strongest engine of freedom in the history of modern society, and it is one of the centre-left's greatest triumphs.

And its goals are still intact.

But the way we manage the public sector is far from static.

Alongside the success we've had in building a public sector, you will also find a justified criticism of bureaucracy and examples of inefficiency. Everything from the exercise of government powers to the provision of services has been subject to criticism in the process of expanding welfare.

Fortunately, various governments, local politicians and other stakeholders have committed to modernising and improving the efficiency of the public sector. Meanwhile, sweeping and marked improvements in today's services have offset many criticisms of the past. In many fields, efficiency and service in the public sector significantly outpace that of other sectors in society.

Nonetheless, there is a realisation and a sense that we need to re-examine management of the public sector and see if we can come up with a new and better foundation. There seems to be a general fatigue and resignation regarding the current management regime in far too many parts of the public sector.

The criticism is extensive and multifaceted, but the focal points are as follows: there is a lack of leadership, there is a lack of certainty in planning, there are no incentives for improved productivity, institutions are subject to budgetary whims, there are no incentives for personal initiative, and there is a lack of coherence between political expectations and budgets.

Let's take a look at a couple of examples: A large municipality has an in-home assistant team of 30 people. The employees figure out how they can rearrange their routes and save 3-5% of the budget. And the reward? One of their colleagues was fired because the administration recouped the improvement in productivity.

In another municipality, more than 10 years of work went into the development and execution of a strategy for youth services, including after-school classes and activity centres, preventive initiatives, etc. All of the plans were approved and everything had been successful and satisfactory. Two weeks before the municipality budget was to be approved, it was announced that the budget must be cut by 30%. How? They didn't care. Why? Because the municipal council had a different view on things than previously.

Yet another municipality has a very active social committee. They frequently enquire about the purchasing policies of individual institutions, including for food, personal care products, etc. The committee is interested in statistics, descriptions and registration – all the way down to the level of individual patients. Result: Institutions and the administration structure their work accordingly, whereby the fulfilment of bureaucracy becomes the central goal of all involved.

Another municipality dedicates countless hours to satisfying the state and Danish Parliament's curiosity about how each employee spends their working time, and to meet detailed demands from departments and various coalitions about progress towards achieving political goals. But it's highly doubtful that these reports are used for anything at all.

The last example for now comes from a municipality's elderly services department, which adopted an excellent plan for service and targets for elderly care. The plan had very good and ambitious goals, and enjoyed broad political support. The problem was that the people who were to execute the plan – management and employees – said that it cannot be done with the allocated resources. The answer they received was that it must be done. They received the allocated resources and not a cent more. And so the management and staff could look forward to numerous complaints about non-compliance with the plan.

<h2 style="text-align:center">A SYSTEM GONE ASTRAY</h2>

New Public Management was the modern fad of the 1990s and sought to introduce top-down management of the public sector with target setting, economic planning and incentives. The core element of this approach is the contract. The more detailed the contract, the more the bureaucracy. In an eye-opening op-ed piece a few years back, some of the key figures in the implementation of this approach (all former employees of the Danish Ministry of Finance) asserted that NPM had gone too far, and that the expected results had largely failed to materialise.

In times past, municipalities and counties in Denmark virtually always had budget overruns. In other words, the public sector grew more than planned. One can certainly claim that this was a reflection of the actual costs, but it was by no means an expedient form of managing public finances. The Danish Budget Act changed the ground rules. The Budget Act provides a precise description of the sanctions to be levied on individual institutions that fail to comply with budgets and financial frameworks. This Act has contributed to the rise of a culture in which budget overruns are rare – and there is very good reason to uphold this culture.

Since the 1990s, great efforts have been made to ensure increased competition, increased supply, an expanded scope of activities subject to competition and increased public procurement – all driven by the ideological edict that the public sector must learn from the private. Oftentimes, these efforts were accompanied by a desire for increased privatisation of welfare and the introduction of insurance programmes, with user payment and an intention of differential treatment between the insured and non-insured. After 30 years of efforts, the results are questionable. Private companies have often enjoyed a brief lifetime in the welfare sector, with their greatest success coming in areas where they were overcompensated compared to their public counterparties. Meanwhile, the required volume of procurement and potential competition have created a bureaucratic monster, financed and borne by the public sector.

Management reform – increased autonomy

The solution for the public sector is not detailed top-down management, ideological crusades for privatisation, nor centralised fiscal controls. These paths have been explored ad nauseam, and there are no examples of countries on this blue planet that have succeeded any better than Denmark.

If the public sector is to chart new paths, it will take a new framework and new political choices.

The key conclusion of the centre-left is that we must create space for management to manage. And this management must be performed by those employed for the task – for the benefit and pleasure of employees and citizens.

This conclusion is actually very far-reaching and, if realised, it would completely transform the way we presently control and manage the public sector.

It would require the political entities – parliament, region or municipality – to operate with a different form of budget control. Specifically, one could envision a model with a four-year agreement stipulating the specific budget for a day care centre or in-home assistant team.

An agreement/contract of this nature would set out the overall objectives for the given task, and delineate the parameters to be assessed and measured. For example, a plan for elderly services in a municipality can provide the basis for the in-home assistant team, but the team will not be measured and have to report on all imaginable aspects of their day-to-day operations. Just a few clear and simple goals, and the rest is the manager's responsibility to figure out.

The price of the task is a specific negotiation. The managers must only accept managerial responsibility if they deem the budget feasible. A manager who does not meet the expectations must then be dismissed.

The contract will also include an agreement as to how surplus funds arising from improved productivity can be used. For example, it could be agreed that two-thirds of the surplus goes to increased wages/welfare for staff, and one-third to the main shareholder, i.e. the public sector; other models are also possible.

The critical thing is that both managers and employees are given incentives to cultivate their innovative and creative ideas, thereby unleashing potential improvements in productivity. This incentive is nowhere to be seen in many parts of today's public sector.

The key to the model's success will be shielding managers (and employees) from the capricious nature of politicians, who constantly meddle in operational issues and impose new demands. An institution, a team, or an area must have a professional managerial reference point, or a board of directors with this responsibility, and as far as possible they should not include elected politicians. Elected politicians must make demands, set goals and prioritise in the process of hammering out contracts, but they must not play an operational role in the public sector. An arm's length principle must reign in the political sphere.

The fiscal control exercised by various public sector bodies must also change. An agreement is an agreement – a principle that will eliminate sudden budget adjustments and reprioritisation from the arsenal of politicians. This means slower fiscal squeezes and stricter requirements for cash reserves in the event of changing market conditions, both of which are logical measures under the Budget Act and framework for fiscal policy. The planning of contracts and agreements is also an ongoing annual process.

We want a public management model in which:
- Institutions, teams and departments are defined as independent bodies as far as possible.
- Independent bodies should ideally have a board or an elected administration.
- A four-year contract/agreement is adopted for each body.
- A four-year budget period is agreed, during which time unused funds can be carried over from year to year.
- New or revised requirements in the contract/agreement trigger corresponding financial compensation.
- No more than three parameters are to be measured. The remainder of goal fulfilment is the responsibility of the manager and board.
- If goals in a contract are not met, the manager can be replaced.
- Productivity gains can be divided 50/50 or 75/25 between personnel bonuses and the municipality.
- The work required to answer time- and resource-intensive questions from public administrators and politicians will be billed.
- The contract/agreement will be renegotiated every four years, with the involvement of politicians and public administrators.
- If the model is not suited for a given area, step on the brakes and find a different way of operating the area.

Reforms of the public sector should not stop here. Through the ages, efforts have been made to establish collaborations between the private and public sectors, and often with great success. The introduction of management and control mechanisms, combined with a focus on the bottom line and capital instruments, has delivered satisfactory results in some cases for owners, managers and employees. A certain degree of private ownership also provides extra protection against public owners suddenly changing terms and conditions without providing additional funding.

First-class service and organisation is found throughout the public sector. In fact, it is so exemplary that it can be sold to other countries. However, Denmark has yet to establish a proper business in this regard, due to the lack of incentives for management and personnel (why should they generate more self-funding, if they don't get anything out of it?), and due to the lack of expertise in establishing a business platform, e.g. for exports.

If we want to pursue a goal of sales and exports of assets generated in the public sector, it would be expedient to seek out a private-public partnership.

Much of the public sector was founded with the benevolent objective of meeting a need rooted in the public interest that the private market either could not, or preferred not to meet. Large parts of the utilities sector are an example of this. For example, waterworks were established throughout Denmark as needed, and on the principle of "resting within themselves", i.e. no pursuit of profit.

The question is whether developments in and around these sectors now require us to think differently going forward? For example, it seems rather strange that Denmark constantly stands out with its exceptional concepts in water technology, but is unable to capitalise on these concepts in the market due to organisational restrictions. The educational sector has seen a blossoming of business-oriented and user-paid programmes of study, enabling educational institutions to generate significant funds, but they are still barred from bringing private capital into the equation.

Of course, this does not apply in every case and to everyone. In some areas, it would be beneficial to bring in private capital – in others, it would be inexpedient.

And in most cases the following can be said: These are more or less natural public monopolies, and in any such endeavour, the majority of shares must remain in the hands of the public sector. A minimum of 51% must be owned by society.

During the 1980s, Thatcher sold off a large share of the social housing stock to the private sector, thus robbing future generations of the right to affordable housing, and stealing capital built up by past generations. The result is a housing sector marred by inequality in the large British cities, pushing ordinary people out in favour of speculators. A certain amount of social housing is a natural public monopoly.

Train services were also privatised, resulting in chaos,

while electricity companies headed by gangsters in the US is the legacy left behind by the egoistic havoc of the liberals.

Denmark sold off its telecommunications infrastructure, and in the year 2017 Danes continue to suffer from a miserable supply of broadband services and mobile coverage, as the private monopoly milks the market.

If parts of natural public monopolies are put up for sale, it's incredibly important that the centre-left ensures that the remaining 51% share is never sold. There must be constitutional protections against such sales – a shield that can stave off a new round of Thatcher/Reagan 2.0, bringing with it policies that could smash and destroy everything we've spent decades building in just a few years' time.

TOLERANCE FOR DIFFERENT APPROACHES

The public sector is actually many different sectors, many different institutions, many different regions and people. What it takes to successfully run a nursing home in Odense is not necessarily the same as for a nursing home in The Hague.

We do not believe that you can concoct the perfect managerial method and organisational structure, just as the idea of the automated hair trimmer capable of serving all of humanity regardless of cranial dimensions is hopefully also an idea definitively put to bed.

Our final principle in this debate is that if instituting the reforms laid out above doesn't make sense, then don't!

The ability to find solutions somewhere in between is a good thing. And if the debate on the public sector of the future gives rise to new and even better ideas, that's great! Our aim is to send the public sector in a direction where we change our administrative approach based on the stated objective of making our public sector better for all involved.

MAIN POINTS

- ✓ The welfare society and its building, the public sector, are inextricably linked and remain a central goal for us.

- ✓ We must institute an autonomy reform that creates room for management to manage. And this management must be performed by those employed for the task, for the benefit and pleasure of employees and citizens.

- ✓ If we want to pursue a goal of sales and exports of assets generated in the public sector, it would be expedient to increase private-public partnerships.

- ✓ In the case of natural public monopolies, the majority of shares must remain in the hands of the public sector. A minimum of 51% must be owned by society.

- ✓ We must have constitutional protection that prevents the sale of natural public monopolies.

PEOPLE AND DRUGS

The most sensible advice that a person can receive is to stay away from stimulants. Live healthy, live well and live simply – and stay far away from alcohol, cigarettes, caffeine, drugs and similar stimulants. All drugs and substances will, to a greater or lesser extent, destroy you physically, socially, financially or mentally. So the good advice is: Don't do it!

But only the fewest actually follow this advice. And it's not because they are unaware. People clearly know about the negative aspects of using stimulants. And nonetheless they do it. This is not just a phenomenon of human civilisation. Excavations of prehistoric sites show that various tribes and societies also used stimulants, the most common of which was alcohol.

Humans will inevitably choose to use stimulants – despite information proposing the opposite.

Although there's probably a biological and psychological explanation for this, that's beyond the expertise of this author – although the politics aren't.

People in power have tried to manage this fact through the ages. The most famous example is prohibition in the United States, which gave rise to both the mafia and Hollywood while it lasted. Prohibition of alcohol also garnered popularity in Scandinavia, particularly in Sweden and Norway.

Our contemporaries typically shake their heads in amazement regarding these measures, but there was actually a good reason for their adoption. Industrialisation and the social degradation of the working class was accompanied by extensive and destructive alcohol abuse amongst workers. The prohibitionists saw a ban on alcohol as a social tool that could protect individuals and their families from the disastrous effects of alcohol abuse. In Sweden and Norway, the prohibition movement went hand in hand with the workers' movement. Only a sober working class would be receptive to a political awakening. To this day, we see the effects of this movement: the monopoly on selling beer and liquor in Sweden and Norway.

The ban actually worked to some extent in Sweden and Norway. Not so much in the US.

Certain religions have attempted to prescribe the stimulants their followers were allowed – or, rather, prohibited – from using. Islam has apparently succeeded in prohibiting alcohol, until those involved find shortcuts to other stimulants or to using alcohol, for example outside of Islamic countries.

But the urges of the powerful to regulate people's use of stimulants doesn't stop here.

Tobacco was welcomed with great joy when the tobacco plant was brought over from South America, and particularly after World War II in the form of cigarettes. Smoking became the norm. Unfortunately, it turned out that this was extremely deadly, and various forms of legislation have since sought to limit people's tobacco consumption. But tobacco is so popular that nobody has yet attempted to prohibit it by law. So, virtually anywhere in the world, you can go into a shop and purchase it legally.

The same tolerance is not exhibited when it comes to other types of drugs. Since the 1960s, when the use of cannabis, LSD, opioids, psychedelic mushrooms, etc. became popular, the powers that be have taken a rigid and intolerant approach to these substances, with only few exceptions. In many parts of the world, the use and possession of even small dosages of drugs can trigger the death penalty. And zero-tolerance is even the basis for a free-spirited country such as Denmark.

Yet people in Denmark and around the world use these various drugs, in spite of the major personal risks from a punitive society.

As we will see in the following, it is doubtful that the hard-line and restrictive approach has had any positive effect.

People are predisposed to seek out stimulants, and it seems that the regulatory efforts of governments only play a secondary role.

This forces us to discuss and assess whether the way we have devised our laws and social initiatives is the right approach.

The dismaying conclusion is that there is no historical evidence, no economic justification, no social justification, and perhaps no moral rationale for our principles of freedom and punishment regarding the use of drugs.

A BRIEF HISTORY

Let's ignore alcohol and cigarettes for a moment and take at look at the illegal substances.

Throughout the past 50 years, we have sought to fight the distribution and consumption of cannabis and other drugs.

Through extensive policing efforts, longer prison sentences, surveillance, information campaigns, and political and moral condemnation, these efforts have been massive and persistent. If you were to add up the resources dedicated to this aim, the sum would be astronomical, regardless of which countries we're talking about.

For example, if someone were to add up the figures on how much the United States spends on police, border control, public prosecutors and prisons, the total would be unfathomable and it's growing year after year. In the 2000s, the United States spent approximately $25 billion annually on drug control efforts. There are currently 500,000 people incarcerated in the US because of drug-related crimes – in 1980, it was 40,000. The more the US punishes, the more expensive it becomes for society – yet the eye-opening conclusion is that it makes zero impact on consumption rates.

In Denmark, every schoolchild knows where you can

buy cannabis in the local neighbourhood. The more inquisitive teenager will also know how to obtain ecstasy and similar drugs. Despite the dedicated efforts of information campaigns, schools, parents, police and assorted public authorities to preach the dangers of using cannabis and other drugs, consumption has remained intact and is perhaps even increasing.

As new episodes continuously arise involving the smuggling of cannabis and narcotics, seizures, etc, the political world has consistently increased the penal framework for smugglers, dealers and consumers of these substances. The result is more people in prison, yet consumption has remained relatively unaffected.

Time and again at Christiania in Copenhagen, the police have attempted to clear the so-called "Pusher Street", where cannabis is openly sold at stands. As long as police clad in riot gear are on the scene, these efforts work. Meanwhile, the cannabis trade relocates to other parts of the city. As soon as the police leave – voilà! – Pusher Street rises from the ashes.

This could be seen as a humorous and comic episode from a day in the life of Copenhagen, if it didn't involve a lot of people whose lives and well-being are put on the line.

It is the duty of legislators to deploy healthy young men and women in uniform to enforce the law. And this often results in violent conflicts, including the deaths of those involved.

This forces legislators to ask themselves whether their priorities are in order. Is it the right thing to do to put police officers' lives on the line to enforce something that cannot be successfully enforced in the long run?

The number of police deaths in the global battle against cannabis and other drugs is incredibly high.

Could one posit that they've sacrificed their lives for a good and reasonable cause? The answer to the former might be yes, but what about the latter?

Through more than 50 years of efforts, the authorities can point to stunningly few lasting successes.

Regardless of escalated efforts – going as far as the death penalty – consumption remains unchanged or rising.

There are no strategies for successfully fighting cannabis and other drugs with more severe punishment and increased police resources.

Denmark's police and customs authorities periodically issue reports on how much cannabis or other drugs they have seized. These reports typically include information about the street value of these drugs. And the figures are mind-boggling. But the authorities typically only succeed in confiscating a very small share of this revenue. The supplies will continue to stream in, regardless of the efforts of the authorities – because there are huge sums to be had in this trade.

At the time of this writing, a new computer game in which you play the role of a Central American drug lord recently hit the market, and there are even popular online series where you can follow along in the daily lives of actual drug lords. Like the gangsters of the prohibition era, they too have been sluiced into the Hollywood entertainment machine. The tales of how Columbia's Pablo Escobar practically financed an entire country and had monthly expenses of $2,500 for rubber bands to bundle his dollar bills are good stories. And they tell you something about how much money is circulating in this industry.

The global value of drug trafficking amounts to $320 billion annually. And the majority of this revenue is generated in the Western world.

Considering the potential to earn so much money, it is quite clear that people around the world are willing to take the risk, no matter the punishment. And those most willing to run these risks are those who already have problems with law and order – the criminal gangs, new and old.

Add to this the people who produce the drugs, who are often impoverished third world farmers with no other attractive sources of income. They too will continue to produce, even though their share of the profits is miniscule.

And the question of finances goes beyond the manufacturers and dealers. Consumers and society also spend vast sums.

THE ADDICT

In Copenhagen on any given weekend, it is hardly difficult to find people in the city's nightclubs who are on some type of drug – and the drug in question is rarely cannabis.

Many people, especially youth, get acquainted with drugs and engage in weekend use. The vast majority keep it at this, and they typically bid drugs adieu when they get older. For them, there are no financial problems associated with buying drugs, and they do not become physically addicted or drug abusers.

Unfortunately, however, some do. Despite the difficulty and varying methods of calculation, it is estimated that 30,000 to 70,000 people in Denmark have a drug abuse problem. Many of them begin by trying cannabis and other drugs, after which they develop a dependence that leads to serious abuse.

They risk a daily life where everything is secondary to the goal of consuming drugs.

The worst of these addictions are seen with drugs such as heroin.

Let's take a closer look at the financial case of the addict. It costs about 500 kroner a day for a seasoned junkie to get heroin.

If you are in need of 500 kroner a day for drugs alone, you are going to need a rather nice monthly salary. And that is something that drug addicts don't have. Or, rather, they actually have a very high income, but it is not earned through standard wage labour. It is generated through criminality or prostitution.

Quite simply, a drug addict needs 182,500 kroner a year in net income for drugs alone. If you need to steal your way to that much money, you have to steal a lot, unless you can get your hands on cash.

On the market for stolen goods, you can usually get

about 10% of the retail price. A television that costs 5,000 kroner in the shops gets you 500 kroner – so by these calculations, you have to steal goods valued at 1,850,000 kroner a year. Denmark's drug addicts are thereby among the nation's absolute elite in terms of annual income.

You can also prostitute yourself for the needed income. At 500 kroner a shot, that means one customer a day, times 365. Yikes.

Denmark has an estimated 13,000 addicts who inject their drugs.

Our policy is to give them methadone, and otherwise 100% zero tolerance (unless they are participating in the medically prescribed heroin scheme). Addicts may have very small amounts of drugs seized and face punishment for the same.

Many heroin addicts live on the streets and often abuse a wide range of other substances as well. The drugs they buy are frequently impure and contain other hazardous substances – so much so that addicts die from overdoses.

Approximately 240 drug addicts die from an OD each year in Denmark.

The picture is the same around the world. Those who become abusers of hard drugs typically have a horrible life and are met by a society that responds with equally callous brutality.

Addicts don't even stop their drug abuse when in prison. It is impossible to keep the prisons drug-free, so addicts find a supply – on the condition that they pay their drug debts once they are released from prison. This just makes it even more difficult for them to succeed in life. A rare few manage to escape from addiction each year – regardless of the extensive programmes dedicated to this aim.

In addition to the social and personal problems associated with drug abuse, addiction to drugs is also a recipe for financial ruin.

The total cost of society's efforts to combat cannabis and other drugs is difficult to calculate.

It's an equation where cause and effect are difficult to register. Is a burglary just a burglary, or is it directly related to drugs? Is the scope and power of organised crime solely due to the sale of drugs?

In Denmark, 16% of all criminal charges are directly connected to offences laid down in the criminal code on narcotics. This includes users, dealers and smugglers.

But what about burglary, for example? Can we assume that the majority of burglaries and theft committed in Denmark is related to junkies seeking goods they can sell to the local fence? The calculation above indicates that this is probably a reasonable conclusion.

Prison staff estimate that around two-thirds of all incarcerations are related to drugs.

And what of violence? How much of it is drug-related?

A news programme by the Danish Broadcasting Corporation estimated that one-third of criminal activity is related to drugs. And that is a very modest estimate, based on the finding that 3.4 billion kroner is spent annually on police efforts to combat drugs.

When you add police efforts to the costs of public prosecutors, courts, prisons, social services, prison administration, hospitals, healthcare professionals, etc, you get a much higher figure.

One could argue that all of this spending is worth every cent in the name of morality. But the claim that it is effective simply doesn't hold water.

THE MORAL HIGH BAR

Regardless of the statistics and state of affairs, punishment and legality remain a question of society's views and moral foundation. Throughout history, societies have had vastly different views on prostitution, ranging from total liberalisation and social acceptance to clerical condemnation and severe punishment.

We do not have much historical experience to draw on in relation to cannabis and other drugs, with the exception perhaps being the Opium Wars, where the Chinese emperor banned opium but the British exerted military force to ensure continued sale for the benefit of their merchants.

As one drug after the next has emerged in society, we have rated it dangerous and banned it. As previously mentioned, the vast majority of countries have a zero tolerance approach to cannabis and other drugs, although these policies are beginning to soften up in some quarters.

But if we were to imagine a general assembly, convened to reassess what we were going to permit – based on the assumption that human beings are sinful by

114

ASSORTED STATISTICS
– ALCOHOL, SMOKING AND DRUG ABUSE

	ALCOHOL[*]	CIGARETTES[*]	CANABIS[*]	HARD DRUGS (injection-abuse)[***]	TOTAL DRUG ABUSE[*]
TOTAL DEATHS, ANNUALLY	2,900	14,000	-	225	**1,000** (400 where drug abuse is the direct cause, and 600 where drug abuse is a contributing factor)
TOTAL ABUSERS (Danes with a harmful consumption of alcohol, smokers and drug addicts)	**585,000** or 8,5% of all danes	Approx. **1.3 million**[**] or 22% of all Danes[**].	**11,000**	**3,000**	**33,000**
TOTAL USERS	**4 mio.**[****] or 88% of Denmark's adult population	-	-	-	-
HEALTH EXPENSES, ANNUALLY (treatment and care)	**400 million DKK**	**10 billion DKK**	-	-	**130 million DKK**
PRODUCTIVITY LOSS, ANNUALLY (sickness absence, early retirement and premature death)	**8 billion DKK**	**34 billion DKK**	-	-	**700 million DKK**

xiv

nature and will continue to seek out and consume stimulants – what would the results of our moral recalibration look like?

So that's what the matrix looks like. Who votes for permitting alcohol and cigarettes, and banning cannabis and hard drugs?

The answer to that question is: pretty much every nation in the world.

Since 2001, the consumption of cannabis and other drugs has been decriminalised in Portugal. This means that persons found to be in possession of cannabis or narcotics for personal consumption are not punished, but instead referred to counselling.

So what does 17 years of experience show us? The number of users has actually declined overall, with a significant decline in the use of hard drugs. The number of addicts has declined.

In the United States, a total of nine states have decided to decriminalise the sale of cannabis. An explosion in the number of users or addicts also failed to materialise in these cases.

The Netherlands has permitted the sale of cannabis in coffee shops for many years. The use of cannabis and the rate of drug addiction is no higher in the Netherlands than in comparable nations.

In 2007, Denmark adopted a policy that long-time drug addicts, i.e. people with significant and years-long heroin abuse, could enrol in a scheme by which they were given free heroin, to be injected under supervision. Just a few years after the initiation of the scheme, it was clear that those involved had virtually abandoned all crime and prostitution. They were also able to build a social life, including a permanent residence. They no longer became ill because of impure drugs. Their worst problems remained their abuse of other substances, particularly alcohol, and the impacts of many years of living on the streets and using impure drugs.

For decision-making politicians, this poses some serious questions about the way we have currently structured our legislation and society.

The first question we should ask ourselves is whether
it is morally just and rationally sensible that we crimi-
nalise people who have become addicted to a substance?

From a moral perspective, you could just as well
argue that these people have a disease of addiction,
and that it would be insanity to continue criminalising
them. These people have but a miniscule chance of escape from their addiction – regardless of the treatment
schemes offered – and further punishing them only
drives them deeper into the abyss of debt, addiction
and criminal and social deviance.

Decriminalise these people and their consumption.
And let's make it possible for people who become addicted to drugs to receive treatment just like other sick
people, i.e. structured assistance and the drugs they
need, rather than leaving them to the streets and the
criminals. Put an end to junkies in the streets and al-
leys – give them instead the assurance of treatment in
structured programmes that enable them to maintain
their social lives.

Such a solution would also decriminalise all of the
other users. Learning from the example of Portugal, we
know there is no need to hesitate. The claim that it will
lead to an increase in drug consumption can be coun-
tered and laid to rest with real world facts. Tasking
the police, courts, public prosecutors, etc with running
after small-time users seems to be an utterly hopeless

and foolish effort. If you want to add education to the equation, we could follow Portugal's lead and institute compulsory counselling.

The next step is legalising cannabis. More than 50 years of combat has led to defeat on all fronts. Consumption remains constant, the supply remains constant, and the flow of money to criminal gangs remains constant. Believing that you can stem the supply and consumption is refusing to pay any heed to the clear evidence offered by reality.

By legalising and thereby organising sales through the state, you can determine who can buy and you gain access to revenue that can serve many good purposes.

First and foremost, legalisation is tantamount to the financial ruin of organised crime. Cannabis sales represent their prime source of income.

And to quench any moral qualms, we could earmark every cent earned on these sales for assisting those who develop an addiction and for informational campaigns on the dangers of drug use. This would enable top-notch research, psychologists, social assistance and information campaigns, which would put our moral bottom line light years ahead of our current allocation of revenue from the taxation of alcohol and cigarettes.

The precise details of how we organise sales can always be adjusted, including punishment for consumers and sellers who circumvent the official channels for procuring cannabis. It would also make much more sense for the police and other authorities to pursue that legal order.

We've grown up with the understanding that taking drugs is most likely the road to sitting in a gutter somewhere with a needle in your arm.

But the validity of that story is simply rubbish.

As detailed above, the number of users is very high and the number of addicts is much lower. There are people who use drugs but never end up addicts as a consequence.

Given this understanding, what in the world are we going to do – politically and morally?

The immediate reaction among friends and colleagues is to disregard the question and say that people can just get drunk instead. In other words, they close their eyes and cover their ears because it's a difficult question to consider.

But wouldn't it be a good idea for us to take on this discussion and think about our courage and ability to take yet another step?

We can do this while acknowledging at the same time that it is incredibly difficult. For example, will we nod approvingly to the prospect of an 18-year-old girl going to the store to buy speed?

Just writing this brings wrinkles to the brow. On the other hand, have we not okayed that she can buy all the alcohol and cigarettes she wants? You can bet your boots we did. And if she really wants some drugs, doesn't she pretty much know where to get them? Yep, she probably does, and that goes for any kind of drugs – heroin, cocaine, speed, you name it.

It's convenient to avoid this discussion, but it's hypocritical to pretend that anything has been solved.

You could also put it this way, from the perspective of parents: Would we rather our children drink massive amounts of alcohol and expose themselves to uncontrollable behaviour, physical injury, etc, or take speed and dance all night long?

Most parents would answer that they prefer alcohol.

Are we certain that this is the right conclusion for the future?

About the discussion

It's not difficult to imagine the reactions that will be triggered in this debate. It's impossible to stay rooted on rational ground when emotions fly through the air like grenades. But let's try to stay there for as long as possible.

Because the reality is grotesque. The fight against cannabis and narcotics is a high priority issue in virtually all countries and has caused a human tragedy exceeding that of most wars. Real people of flesh and blood are dying in the streets – in connection with police work and in prisons – and the situation increasingly resembles the hopeless trench warfare of WWI. The war against cannabis and narcotics has gone on for nearly sixty years. The victims and the losses are enormous.

We, the centre-left, must take the lead in this discussion and attempt to limit the intensity and scope of this insanity. Along the way, we will be met with condemnation, suspicion and victims who will be used and mis-used in all respects. Seek a return to rationality in every case – this is where we can do the most for humankind.

Main points

✓ Humans will inevitably choose to use stimulants – despite information proposing the opposite.

✓ The authorities, police and others are tasked with an impossible mission every day. Our prisons are primarily full of people whose crime is rooted in the use of cannabis and other drugs.

✓ Our zero tolerance on cannabis and other drugs is a total failure. It doesn't work and has only resulted in more victims and higher costs. The disaster is of epic proportions, in both human and financial terms.

✓ The current state of affairs channels extensive financial means to criminals, and the authorities only have very limited success in preventing this enrichment.

✓ The use of cannabis and other drugs must be decriminalised. It no longer makes any sense to pursue a zero tolerance policy.

✓ Legalise cannabis and ensure controlled sales by the

state, and channel the revenue from these sales to those negatively impacted by drug use.

✓ Start the discussion and lay the groundwork for further steps towards legalising some of the other substances.

✓ Provide controlled treatment to all those who become addicted to drugs, allowing them free access to drugs or similar treatment.

THE PUBLIC CONVERSATION

Journalism

The most difficult and touchy profession you can start a discussion about is journalism. At the first signs of criticism, they wail like stuck pigs and douse the flames with constitutions, freedom of expression, abuse of power and self-righteousness, after which they typically conclude that they were right (as usual). A piece of good advice is to avoid criticising journalists, but since they are very much a part of the problem, this is also good advice worth ignoring.

THE DISAPPEARANCE OF REGULAR REPORTING

If there's one thing that can invoke a political journalist's ire, it's a colleague who is just "a nodding head". Giving coverage to what a politician actually says without editing is seen as a journalistic defeat. This follows from a perception of politicians as manipulative, tactical and dishonest, whereby it is the role of the journalist to "unveil" and edit the true reality. And thus follows the assumption of journalists that they cannot leave it to readers or viewers to judge for themselves.

This is the quintessential attitude of political journalists in Denmark. There are, of course, exceptions to the rule.

But the above is a good representation of the status quo, as materialised in two discouraging phenomena:

123

First, politicians and other public figures respond to this journalistic approach by taking a number of precautions. They shield themselves and want to know what "angle" the journalist is working on before they will comment. And by angle, they mean the headline and premise of the story. If it's in your favour, then fine; if not, then less fine. Almost regardless of what you say, you cannot get the journalist to change his or her angle. The journalist thus becomes a medium, for example between two political press departments who are fighting for an advantage and favourable angle. Quotes given to the press are edited according to what side of the angle the interview subject is situated. In many cases, you're better served by not participating in the process, which at least prevents your being misused in that context.

Political journalism thus becomes a game in which tactical positioning, often accompanied by personalised messages, is the key product in itself, and actually has very little to do with a party's actual positions and views. Political reporting has become a tactical swamp, with journalists in the starring role.

Readers and viewers are subjected to this product. And their reaction is clear: People are fleeing from this coverage, not interested in reading, viewing or buying any of it.

The second discouraging phenomenon: People out there never learn what a party or a politician actually stands for. If, for example, the Social Democrats announce a proposal on youth education programmes, it is unlikely to get any coverage – unless, that is, it is accompanied by conflict or personal intrigue, in which case only the part about the conflict will be covered.

So where does that leave the people of society? With no knowledge and no way of becoming informed about the various parties' political proposals, unless they seek such information elsewhere.

It's surprising that this massive decline in readers and viewers hasn't caused the press to consider that the thing they've abandoned is basic reporting – reporting that is fair to the person or organisation being covered, while giving voice to opposing views, but waiting until the second or third round of coverage to analyse and judge.

Politicians are constantly being asked why we never hear from them, or why they don't argue on television like they do in the town hall. The answer is very simple: On television, you are often edited down to 10 seconds, because afterwards a political editor is going to spend two minutes telling people what the politician actually believes. All politicians are aware of the 10 second policy, so the answers they give to television journalists are typically parrot answers. They give the same answer, no matter what they are asked, and they have rehearsed it in advance; because if you answer incorrectly in the slightest, or employ longer chains of logic, you'll be edited and projected as an idiot. Given the choices, the parrot wins out.

Political journalism has leap-frogged reporting and gone directly to the judgement and analysis. And therefore the most burning desire of many journalists is to become a political analyst, so they can free themselves entirely of having to report on anything that politicians say or believe.

THE CULTURAL MELTDOWN OF JOURNALISM

In connection with the 2015 parliamentary elections in Denmark, many residents of southern Jutland voted for the Danish People's Party. This caused a wide range of media to send reporters to the region and examine how in the world they could have come up with that idea. It was comic to see how the reporters went to work like anthropologists, on a scale not seen since Tintin ventured into the Congo.

But it also revealed that the Copenhagen-based media and their journalists know zilch about the province and the countryside – about the lives, views and values of the people who live there. And it appears to be a common trend internationally. The established press in the United States apparently still can't fathom how people could vote as they did in the 2016 presidential elections.

In today's society, it's apparently possible to live an isolated life within the same country, with communications professionals ensconced in the logic of the big city and devoid of the slightest contact with life outside their metropolitan bubbles. And thus it is that they confuse their daily problems and challenges with those of the population at large. This is how the shortage of organic baby bottles in central Copenhagen becomes a bigger issue than the closing of a pharmacy in the town of Vojens.

Journalists and media have become a big city phenomenon with its own views and values, which are typically elitist. One of the most humorous episodes of recent times was when politicians proposed transferring a Copenhagen radio station (which is 100% state-subsidised) to Jutland. The rage amongst journalists seemingly knew no end...

The claim that journalists are performing a public service is a doubtful one.

In the heart of the beast

Tabloid journalism is one of the specialties of the press. Hard-hitting headlines and scandalous photos are the preferred instruments, with the subjects – or rather, victims – typically being famous people. Countless are the stories of famous figures who are portrayed in libellous articles or ruthlessly harassed in their private lives. Apparently, these types of stories are big sellers, so they continue to be published ad infinitum.

The assertion is that a person who has chosen to be a public figure of his or her own accord, and perhaps even used the press along the way, must accept media coverage good and bad. And, of course, that is a ludicrous excuse, as only the fewest public figures have sought fame through the media. Actors, footballers, the royal family, TV hosts, politicians, etc are not TV reality products (or 99% of them aren't in any case).

Nonetheless, they must accept harsh treatment, direct lies and orchestrated manipulation regarding their professional and private lives. Throughout the Western world, predominantly right-wing media agencies fill their coffers with this systematic and cynical drudgery. They do it because it pays, and there are virtually no consequences for publishing lies. Perhaps a small fine or a wagging finger from the courts, but the publishers can laugh all the way to the bank in the face of these feeble reprimands.

Could we imagine, for example, that journalists published accusations of violence, drug dealing and rape by a named policeman, after which it all proved to be pure lies and fabrication? That the innocent man and his family lost their jobs, suffered profound psychological trauma and were left to their own devices? And to top it all off, the journalists were just hired by another media company and continued their style and genre, while enjoying promotions to leading positions? Time and again, they lie and deceive, while a little tsk-tsk here or there from the Press Council (whose members are the press themselves) never hurt a bit. Thus, the state of law, prosecutors, judges and morality are all left to be processed in the heart of a beast, whose only repentance is a few strategic crocodile tears here and there.

Or what about openly accusing a cancer doctor, by name, of experimenting on patients and proclaiming him guilty as judge and jury – and now, seven years later, the journalist still has the same job and a big smile on his face as the studio host of a new programme? Oh yes. And the victim? Who cares?

Thus, under cover of the freedom of the press, the

same evil is exercised in Denmark, England, the United States and elsewhere.

It must stop. It cannot be true that this tyranny can continue with zero consequences. Instead, they must be subject to significant fines, e.g. the revenue from a full day's sales of a libellous front page story, while journalists and editors are held personally liable. And it must be actual judges who consider the charges and levy the punishment.

Everyone who is subject to unjust attacks – including public figures – is entitled to legal recourse, and we must institute a regulatory framework for the conduct of tabloid journalists and publications.

THE RETURN OF THE PARTY PRESS

One day one of the large English football clubs had enough. Once again, one of their squad was on the front pages of the tabloid press, steamrolled by a journalist who used the smallest straw in the haystack of an interview to cause an uproar. So, the club simply decided that they would begin producing their own stories about their footballers, using their own journalists, photographers and editors. And people could choose whether or not to read the coverage, because it was posted online for free.

Naturally, this didn't stop the tabloid press from continuing their dirty ways, but at least the club conveyed their own messages and were able to shield young footballers in their squad from the tabloid press.

The political parties have begun to emulate this

model. Since the established press no longer reports on the actual views of the parties, they must take matters into their own hands. And the internet makes it all rather inexpensive and quite simple.

The parties are thus the publishers of a unique product, because no other outlet loyally covers their positions. This content is attractive to those who want to stay abreast of the party's political messages – including those who support the party, their opposition, and those with a general interest in politics.

And people read and view this content with a clear understanding that the sender is the party itself, and thus that the level of self-criticism will be limited.

If it gets too nauseatingly propagandistic, people will tune out. If a decent and sober tone is maintained, people will continue reading it, and it will thereby provide an important service to the public. The more readers and viewers, the happier the parties, so there is good reason to keep it nice and proper.

And thus we see the reawakening of the party press, forcing the established press once again to acknowledge that it cannot completely fulfil its public service obligation.

SoMe – Code of conduct

Using Facebook can be a brutal experience. As a politician, you're used to a bit of everything, but reading through the comments of random users can leave even the thickest-skinned of us in a depressed state. It's amazing how biting, degrading and hateful the comments people write online are. In fact, it's absolutely mind-blowing. We're talking about people from all walks of life, with all sorts of educational backgrounds, from all over the country and from every profession imaginable.

Just think if we talked to each other like that when we interacted on the train or in the streets.

In analogue life, we actually have laws and rules about how we must behave towards each other. You can be fined for libel, slander and defamation of character. But online, it seems, anything goes.

Given that nobody is particularly concerned about the health and well-being of politicians, let's instead take a look at the conduct of children and young people towards each other online. What we find is just as abhorrent and irresponsible. People are engaging in pure evil, and nobody is stopping them. The victims are many, and the damage is serious.

The reports we read on young people's low self-esteem, stress and mood swings are largely associated with their experiences on social media. The brutality is unprecedented, because so many people can join in, and because so many people lose their minds when sitting alone with their smartphones.

This cannot go on untethered.

We must establish some rules for proper conduct, together with some filters that protect us.

Some will claim that this is a task of Sisyphean dimensions, and that new forums will continue to sprout up and invite renewed harassment. It is true that we cannot eradicate all the stupidity and offensive behaviour for time immemorial, but we can certainly curb the scope of it. In any case, we should try.

A simple method could be some kind of standardised self-certification, by which users accept or sign off on a code of conduct. This could include a pledge to refrain from bullying, offensive statements of disapproval, saying disparaging things about others, making racist, homophobic comments, etc. If you sign off on a standard code of conduct, you can filter your social media so that you are only in a network and circle of friends with others who have signed off on it as well. Violation of the code of conduct triggers a ban from interaction with others who have approved it. User groups will mete out justice by considering complaints about violations.

Is this even feasible in terms of technology and administration? Yes, it is, but it requires the cooperation of the leading social media companies. For example, they have been very strict about preventing pornography and sex, so why not this as well? And with the enormous profits they reap, they should also be able to afford such efforts.

Alternatively, legislation could be introduced, whereby we force the social media companies to prevent discrimination, bullying, racism, etc.

A decent society must protect its citizens from attacks, both physical and verbal. A verbal lawlessness reigns at present – and we have to make sure that it comes to an end.

Main points

✓ Political journalism has become a game, with the journalist in the starring role. Standard political reporting is a dying breed.

✓ People are fleeing from reading and buying today's journalism.

✓ Journalists and media have become a big city phenomenon with its own views and values, which are typically elitist.

✓ The lies and methods of the tabloid press have poisoned the public sphere.

✓ Significant fines and punishment must be doled out to tabloids for their lies and campaigns.

✓ The party press has made a comeback because the parties publish unique content, given that no other outlet loyally covers their positions.

✓ Social media has given rise to a brutal, unpleasant and hateful tone of speech. We must establish some rules for proper conduct, combined with some filters that protect and uphold decent and respectful conversation in the public sphere.

ISRAEL

– a cause for the centre-left

If, in the decades following WWII, you had told Western leftist intellectuals that 60 years later it would be necessary to write an appeal to the centre-left to cull support for the Jewish state, they would have been incredulous.

In the wake of the horrors of the Holocaust, and after the pogroms of the preceding 100 years throughout Europe, the epitome of centre-left indignation was its dedication to building support for the nation of the Jews, Israel. A nation where they could feel safe for the first time in thousands of years.

But, of course, they couldn't.

From the outset, there was resistance from various fronts, followed by a long series of conflicts. Even the Western nations proved of little assistance at times. But with survivors of the horrors of Hitler among their ranks, they built a state modelled on the norms of democratic socialism of that era. Trade unionist Ben Gurion declared the new democracy and the new rule of law – and it has been a democracy with a rule of law ever since.

But the Israelis get no peace. Time and again, they are attacked by Arab neighbours; but fortunately, Israel applies its deft to win these wars. And in the beginning, there was great support for the Jewish state.

134

But this sympathy began to take a turn in the 1970s and 80s. Arabs, Palestinians, are seen as victims and Israel as the oppressive superpower. Despite Palestinian autonomy, unending peace talks, massive Arabic terror and new wars, the conflict between Israelis and Palestinians continues unabated to the present day.

And many of those in the centre-left have arrived at the conclusion that the only way to peace in the Middle East, the Arab countries, is the mother of all conflicts: the conflict between Israel and the Palestinians. In other words, that this would cause Iraq and Iran to stop shooting each other. That various Arab nations would stop oppressing the Kurds. That democracy would blossom in Saudi Arabia and Qatar, and that they would cease treating Palestinians like slave labourers. And the list goes on: a cure for anti-democratic governments, human rights violations, lack of rule of law, and involvement is terror. It would be fantastic if all this were solved by a lasting, peaceful, two-state solution between Israel and the Palestinians – but how likely is that?

Israel covers a very small geographical area, and has a population of 7.5 million. Therefore, it is rather difficult to understand how they are the ones preventing all forms of progress in the rest of the Arab world.

The fact of the matter is that the rest of the Arab world is filled with despotic kleptocrats who have delivered infinitesimally few advances for the broad population over the last 70 years, choosing instead to channel all the revenue, stemming primarily from oil, into the pockets of a narrow elite. Meanwhile, the collective consciousness in the Arab world subscribes to the notion that they are victims and subject to all manner of conspiracy orchestrated by the United States and Israel. It's a convenient explanation of their own incompetence and, combined with the bad habits of a medieval faith, you've got the recipe for the malaise in which they live.

But, unfortunately, the Arabs have gained ever-growing support among the centre-left for their position – presumably due to Israel's prompt handling of wars and terror. But it's a wrong position, and it's doing all the causes for a better world a disservice.

People will not stop fleeing from the Arab countries to the West until they are ensured better living conditions, decent welfare, employment and a social safety net. This requires the countries to fix the problem of their despots, institute the rule of law, ensure proper distribution and preferably democracy, and to wave goodbye to radicalised forms of Islam as the guiding precepts for the fabric of their society. Israel is not preventing them from doing any of these things.

Israel has elections. It's possible that the centre-left isn't always pleased with the results, but a new chance comes along four years later. And between these elections, there is an opposition that can challenge the powers that be. And there is a supreme court that is not bashful about sentencing former politicians to prison if they get caught up in corruption scandals. There is employment, industriousness, research, art and culture. Israel is a modern, democratic welfare state inspired by the Western European model, and it is surrounded by hostile, despotic Arab states.

Israel deserves our support, not the opposite. The right to have a place on this Earth where the Jewish people can live in peace remains a key cause of the centre-left.

And the centre-left in Israel particularly deserves our support. Part of the solution for a lasting peace for the Jewish people is also that we extend our political, trade and military relations, thus giving the Israeli people a reassurance that they will not be left on their own in the event of new conflicts or aggressions. And here, the centre-left's values of freedom, equality and solidarity must be the focal point for a strong new cooperation, in which we could extend our security policy guarantee to include Israeli membership of NATO, and our trade policy to include membership of the European Union.

ISRAEL AS A ROLE MODEL

If developments should shift and the Arab states and their leaders decide to chart a course towards democracy, prosperity and welfare, it will require sweeping and difficult steps, combined with copious investment and organisation. Fortunately, the help and inspiration they need is right in front of them. If anybody has experience in transforming a golden stretch of sand into an effective market economy, it's Israel. Desalination of water, cultivation of the earth, construction of infrastructure of all kinds, the formation of state and bureaucracy, establishment of a welfare state, universities, etc – right there amongst them, on a little stretch of land, all of these things have been achieved.

The Arab countries actually have a much stronger starting point in terms of material and natural resources. All they have to do is roll up their sleeves and get to work.

Israel's many mistakes

Can the centre-left pay unequivocal homage to Israel?

No, of course not. Nations make mistakes, and nations are comprised of many different people with many different views, intentions and goals. This goes for people who live in Belgium, even though not many people spend time condemning Belgium, and it also goes for Israel.

There is every reason in the world to distance ourselves from religious fundamentalists, who plague political life and the daily lives of many ordinary people. We must especially condemn those who whispered in the ear of Rabin's assassin that he did the Israeli people a favour. There is also reason to be deeply sceptical of rabid settlers who take what does not belong to them in the name of God. Even worse are the right wing politicians who discreetly encourage additional settlements and then lie about it publicly. It's horrific to see the brutality manifested at the border checkpoints, where soldiers and authorities behave hideously and disparagingly towards Palestinians. It's sad to listen to the rhetoric of the far right as it mobilises and radicalises public opinion.

And the sometimes disproportionate use of force as a solution is awful and at times incomprehensible.

The good thing is that all of these views are represented in Israel. They are part of the public debate, and people are allowed to voice these views.

Many good centre-left forces in Israel are fighting a daily battle to maintain order and dignity in the midst of an escalating conflict. These admirable efforts deserve our full support. Brutality and abuses have their limits. Israel sometimes exceeds this limit. Only by supporting Israel and the good forces therein can we help Israel remain on a foundation of democracy, humanism and the rule of law – and in this regard, the centre-left can play a leading role.

EXODUS

At the time of this writing, the SPD only has 17% of the German voters' support in a poll. Helmut Schmidt's, Willy Brandt's, Gerhard Schröder's party is headed for a downfall, which, in keeping with tradition, is accompanied by strange internal fractions. In Poland, the Social Democracy of Poland party isn't even represented in the parliament. In Spain, they play second fiddle, and in Greece they are no more. The once omnipotent Swedish Social Democratic Party is fighting to prevent the Sweden Democrats from passing them in the polls.

Portugal and Italy can find comfort in continued social democratic influence, but who knows how long that will last in Italy?

Deep crisis abounds virtually everywhere.

Countries are different and so too are parties, but it is impossible to deny that the centre-left has been extremely hard hit in the past decade. The centre-left has gone from a defining pillar of society to irrelevance in the eyes of citizens. It has been a tragic trek.

My message in this book is that the centre-left has erred and misread the great immigration of Muslims in particular, and that the defining leaders have lost all respect for their traditional voters.

And my assertion is that the centre-left lacks a convincing narrative and ability to mobilise the necessary aggression towards extreme inequality, and instead allows itself to be enchanted by the siren song of globalisation. In this book, I offer an answer to how this task should be tackled. And how we can build further on the finest and most successful elements of the third way, in partnership with the productive business community, and how we can maintain and develop a modern public sector. And why health and education must be our recognised middle names wherever we go. And how this world's predominant crime, drugs, must be addressed by new means if we are to prevent continued human and economic suffering under a long-failed strategy of prohibition. And why the centre-left must stop showering hate on Israel, but instead open its eyes to the real criminals in the international world.

It is not a complete and finalised roadmap. It is a sketch that can be edited, redesigned and developed, and where more talented people than myself can fill the canvas with relevant analyses and specific policies on everything from environment and climate, to social policy, equality, international trade, fiscal policy, and whatever else is needed to make the picture complete. I hope that as many people as possible will contribute to this process – and hopefully with a respect for the heritage which they are carrying forward into the future. The fundamental principles – the pillars – on which democratic socialism rests will never crumble. But parties will, if you do not care for them properly.

Throughout the Western world, one centre-left party after the next has succumbed to internal disputes, as hot-tempered fractions pound each other and the party almost to death. Or, in other cases, less savoury characters have given in to the dreadful temptations of corruption, destroying their party and cause for the sake of personal enrichment. The centre-left seems to have a special talent for entertaining the public with internal tussles and intrigues. But the fact is that it just won't do. The times when voters found such drama festive and still voted for the centre-left are over. If we can't control ourselves, we will never be allowed to rule a country. The centre-left must embrace this challenge and establish party cultures and leadership structures tailored for the present.

One example of that is this book. If it is received with curiosity and an open mind – even if you may disagree with parts of it – then the project has succeeded. If it is received with rage and condemnation, it would be disappointing, but not much of a surprise in a historical context.

Hopefully, the book will be used – not abused – and help to launch a new and progressive movement that seeks to deliver excellent new results for people in the name of the centre-left. Because that is the aim of this book.

Henrik Sass Larsen

"Marmoream relinquo, quam latericiam accepi."

NOTES

i   http://www.pewforum.org/2017/11/29/europes-growing-muslim-population/

ii   http://www.pewforum.org/2017/11/29/europes-growing-muslim-population/

iii   Statistics Denmark, 2016, Ministry for Economic Affairs and the Interior, posters 2016

iv   The Economic Council of the Labour Movement

v   http://nordic.businessinsider.com/highest-paid-ceos-2016-2017-5

vi   UN, Danmarks Nationalbank

vii   Sara Menker on TED.com

viii   Statistics Denmark, the Economic Council of the Labour Movement

ix   www.b.dk/politiko/millionaeren-martin-thorborg-boede-fire-aar-i-usa-og-vendte-tilbage-med-en-opsang

x   Drug Enforcement Agency, US

xi   UN

xii   http://www.stofbladet.dk/6storage/586/51/stof_25.54-59.pdf, https://www.sst.dk/da/sundhed-og-livsstil/~/media/07101779 E7554638B36EEDBC00234590.ashx

xiii   DR3, på stoffer [on drugs], https://www.youtube.com/watch?v=x-J9YPPK4m4Y

xiv   *   Source: The Danish Health Authority (2016), Sygdomsbyrden i Danmark – Risikofaktorer [Disease burden in Denmark]. http://www.si-folkesundhed.dk/upload/2016._risikofaktorer._sygdomsbyrden_i_danmark.pdf

    **   Source: The Danish Health Authority (2017), Danskernes Rygevaner [Smoking habits of Danes]. https://www.sst.dk/da/udgivelser/2018/danskernes-rygevaner-2017

    ***   Source: The Danish Health Authority (2017), Narkotikasituationen i Danmark [Narcotics situation in Denmark]. https://www.sst.dk/da/udgivelser/2017/~/media/AA63B6154AE-A4587A773FC6DDD7FDA12.ashx

    ****   Source: The Danish Health Authority(2014), Danskernes Sundhed – Den nationale sundhedsprofil 2013 [The health of Danes – National health profile]. https://www.sst.dk/da/planlaegning/kommuner/konference-danskernes-sundhed-den-nationale-sundhedsprofil,-6-marts-2018/~/media/1529A4BCF9C64905BAC650B6C45B72A5.ashx

xv   EMCDDA, Drug report Portugal 2017

xvi   https://www.sst.dk/da/nyheder/2013/ordningen-med-laegeordineret-heroin-er-en-succes